Building Systems (BS)

ARE Mock Exam (Architect Registration Exam)

ARE Overview, Exam Prep Tips,
Multiple-Choice Questions and Graphic Vignettes,
Solutions and Explanations

Gang Chen

ArchiteG®, Inc.
Irvine, California

Building Systems (BS) ARE Mock Exam (Architect Registration Exam): ARE Overview, Exam Prep Tips, Multiple-Choice Questions and Graphic Vignettes, Solutions and Explanations

Copyright © 2011   Gang Chen
V1.7   Incorporated minor revisions on 1/3/2015
Cover Photo © 2011   Gang Chen

Copy Editor: Penny L Kortje

ArchiteG®, Inc.
http://www.ArchiteG.com

ISBN: 978-1-61265-003-6

PRINTED IN THE UNITED STATES OF AMERICA

Dedication

To my parents, Zhuixian and Yugen,
my wife, Xiaojie, and my daughters,
Alice, Angela, Amy, and Athena.

Disclaimer

Building Systems (BS) ARE Mock Exam (Architect Registration Exam) provides general information about Architect Registration Exam. The book is sold with the understanding that neither the publisher nor the authors are providing legal, accounting, or other professional services. If legal, accounting, or other professional services are required, seek the assistance of a competent professional firm.

The purpose of this publication is not to reprint the content of all other available texts on the subject. You are urged to read other materials and tailor them to fit your needs.

Great effort has been taken to make this resource as complete and accurate as possible. However, nobody is perfect and there may be typographical errors or other mistakes present. You should use this book as a general guide and not as the ultimate source on this subject. If you find any potential errors, please send an e-mail to:
info@ArchiteG.com

Building Systems (BS) ARE Mock Exam (Architect Registration Exam) is intended to provide general, entertaining, informative, educational, and enlightening content. Neither the publisher nor the authors shall be liable to anyone or any entity for any loss or damages, or alleged loss or damages, caused directly or indirectly by the content of this book.

If you do not wish to be bound by the above, you may return this book to the publisher for a full refund.

Legal Notice

How to Use This Book

We suggest you read *Building Systems (BS) ARE Mock Exam (Architect Registration Exam)* at least three times:

Read once and cover chapter one, two, appendixes, the related FREE PDF files, and other resources. Highlight any information you are not familiar with.

Read a second and third time, focusing on the previously highlighted material and memorize. Repeat this process as many times as you want until you master the content of the book.

After reviewing these materials, you can take the mock exam, and then check your answers and explanations in the back. Make sure to read the explanations for questions you answered correctly, as you may have done so for the wrong reason. Once again, highlight any unfamiliar information.

Like the real exam, the mock exam includes three types of questions: Select the correct answer, check all that apply, and fill in the blank.

Review your highlighted information, and take the mock exam again. Try to answer 100% of the questions correctly this time. Repeat the process until you can answer all the questions correctly.

You should take the mock exam anytime from two weeks to three days before your scheduled exam. Do NOT wait until the night before the real exam. If you do not do well, you will go into panic mode and will NOT have enough time to review your weaknesses.

Read for the final time the night before the real exam. Review ONLY the information you highlighted, especially the questions you did not answer correctly when you took the mock exam for the first time.

One important tip for passing the graphic vignette section of the ARE BS division is to become VERY familiar with the commands of the NCARB software. Many people fail the exam simply because they are NOT familiar with this software and cannot finish the graphic vignette section within the time limit.

For the graphic vignette section, we included a step-by-step solution using screen-shots from the NCARB practice program so that you can use the book to become familiar with the commands, even when you do NOT have a computer in front of you. This book is also very light and you can carry it around easily. These two features will allow you to review the graphic vignette section whenever you have a few minutes.

All commands are described in an **abbreviated manner**. For example, **Draw > Finished Ceiling** means go to the menu on the left hand side of your computer screen, click **Draw,** and then click **Ceiling** to draw the ceiling. This is typical for ALL commands throughout the book.

The Table of Contents is very detailed so you can locate information quickly. If you are on a tight schedule, you can forgo reading the book linearly and jump around to the sections you need.

All our books, including "ARE Mock Exams Series" and "LEED Exam Guides Series," are available at
GreenExamEducation.com

Check out FREE tips and info at **GeeForum.com**, you can post your questions or vignettes for other users' review and responses.

Table of Contents

Chapter One   Overview of the Architect Registration Exam (ARE)

   1. Important links to FREE and official NCARB documents
   2. A detailed list and brief description of FREE PDF files that can be downloaded from NCARB
      - ARE Guidelines
      - NCARB Education Guidelines
      - Intern Development Program Guidelines
      - IDP Supervisor Guidelines
      - Handbook for Interns and Architects
      - Official exam guide, references index, and practice program (NCARB software) for each ARE division
      - The Burning Question: Why Do We Need ARE Anyway?
      - Defining Your Moral Compass
      - Rules of Conduct

   1. What is IDP?
   2. Who qualifies as an intern?

   1. How to qualify for the ARE
   2. How to qualify for an architect license
   3. What is the purpose of the ARE?
   4. What is NCARB's rolling clock?
   5. How to register for an ARE exam
   6. How early do I need to arrive at the test center?

7. Exam format &time
    * Programming, Planning & Practice
    * Site Planning & Design
    * Building Design & Construction Systems
    * Schematic Design
    * Structural Systems
    * Building Systems
    * Construction Documents and Service
8. How are ARE scores reported?
9. Is there a fixed percentage of candidates who pass the ARE exams?
10. When can I retake a failed ARE division?
11. How much time do I need to prepare for each ARE division?
12. Which ARE division should I take first?
13. ARE exam prep and test-taking tips
14. English system (English or inch-pound units) versus metric system (SI units)
15. Codes and standards used in this book
16. Where can I find study materials on architectural history?

Chapter Two   **Building Systems (BS) Division**

Chapter One

Overview of the Architect Registration Exam (ARE)

A. First Things First: Go to the website of your architectural registration board and read all the requirements for obtaining an architect license in your jurisdiction.
See the following link:
http://www.ncarb.org/Getting-an-Initial-License/Registration-Board-Requirements.aspx

B. Download and Review the Latest ARE Documents at the NCARB Website.

1. Important links to FREE and official NCARB documents
The current version of Architect Registration Exam includes seven divisions:

- Programming, Planning & Practice
- Site Planning & Design
- Building Design & Construction Systems
- Schematic Design
- Structural Systems
- Building Systems
- Construction Documents and Services

Note: Starting July 2010, the 2007 AIA Documents apply to all ARE exams.

Six ARE divisions have a multiple-choice section and a graphic vignette section. The Schematic Design division has NO multiple-choice questions, but two graphic vignette sections.

For the vignette section, you need to complete the following graphic vignette(s) based on the ARE division you are taking:

Programming, Planning & Practice
Site Zoning

Site Planning & Design
Site Grading
Site Design

Building Design & Construction Systems
Accessibility/Ramp
Stair Design
Roof Plan

Schematic Design
Interior Layout
Building Layout

Structural Systems
Structural Layout

Building Systems
Mechanical & Electrical Plan

Construction Documents & Services
Building Section

There is a tremendous amount of valuable information covering every step of becoming an architect available free of charge at the NCARB website:
http://www.ncarb.org/

For example, you can find the education guide regarding professional architectural degree programs accredited by the National Architectural Accrediting Board (NAAB), NCARB's Intern Development Program (IDP) guides, initial license, certification and reciprocity, continuing education, etc. These documents explain how you can qualify to take the Architect Registration Exam.

I find the official ARE Guidelines, exam guide, and practice program for each of the ARE divisions extremely valuable. See the following link:
http://www.ncarb.org/ARE/Preparing-for-the-ARE.aspx

Definitely start by studying the official exam guide and practice program for the ARE division you are taking.

2. **A detailed list and brief description of FREE PDF files that can be downloaded from NCARB**
   The following is a detailed list of FREE PDF files you can download from NCARB. They are listed in order based on their importance.

   • **ARE Guidelines** includes extremely valuable information on the ARE overview, six steps to complete ARE, multiple-choice section, graphic vignette section, exam format, scheduling, sample exam computer screens, links to other FREE NCARB PDF files, practice software for graphic vignettes, etc. Read this <u>at least twice</u>.

   • **NCARB Education Guidelines** (Skimming through this should be adequate.)

- **Intern Development Program Guidelines** contains important information on IDP overview, IDP steps, IDP reporting, IDP basics, work settings, training requirements, supplementary education (core), supplementary education (elective), core competences, next steps, and appendices. Most of NCARB's 54-member boards have adopted the IDP as a prerequisite for initial architect licensure. Thus, you should be familiar with it. IDP costs $350 for the first three years, and then $75 annually. The fees are subject to change, and you should always check the NCARB website for the latest information. Your IDP experience is reported at least every six months and within two months of completion for each reporting period (the **Six-Month Rule**). Read this at least twice.

- **The IDP Supervisor Guidelines** (Skimming through this should be adequate. You should also forward a copy of this PDF file to your IDP supervisor.)

- **Handbook for Interns and Architects** (Skimming through this should be adequate)

- **Official exam guide, references index, and practice program (NCARB software) for each ARE division**
  This includes specific information for each ARE division. (Focus on the documents related to the ARE divisions you are currently taking and read them at least twice. Make sure you install the practice program and become very familiar with it. The real exam is VERY similar to this program.)

  a. **Programming, Planning & Practice (PPP)**: Official exam guide and practice program for the PPP division
  b. **Site Planning & Design (SPD)**: Official exam guide and practice program (computer software) for the SPD division
  c. **Building Design & Construction Systems (BDCS)**: Official exam guide and practice program for the BDCS division
  d. **Schematic Design (SD)**: Official exam guide and practice program for the SD division
  e. **Structural Systems (SS)**: Official exam guide, references index, and practice program for the SS division
  f. **Building Systems (BS)**: Official exam guide and practice program for the BS division
  g. **Construction Documents and Services (CDS)**: Official exam guide and practice program for the CDS division

- **The Burning Question: Why Do We Need ARE Anyway?** (Skimming through this should be adequate.)

- **Defining Your Moral Compass** (Skimming through this should be adequate.)

- **Rules of Conduct** is available as a FREE PDF file at:
  http://www.ncarb.org/
  (Skimming through this should be adequate.)

C. The Intern Development Program (IDP)

1. What is IDP?

IDP is a comprehensive training program jointly developed by the National Council of Architectural Registration Boards (NCARB) and the American Institute of Architects (AIA) to ensure that interns obtain the necessary skills and knowledge to practice architecture <u>independently</u>.

2. Who qualifies as an intern?

Per NCARB, an individual can qualify as an intern if s/he is considered one of the following:

a. A graduate from an NAAB-accredited program

b. An architecture student acquiring acceptable training prior to graduation

c. Another qualified individual as identified by a registration board

D. Overview of the Architect Registration Exam (ARE)

1. How to qualify for the ARE

A candidate needs to qualify for the ARE via one of NCARB's member registration boards, or one of the Canadian provincial architectural associations.

Check with your Board of Architecture for specific requirements.

For example, in California, a candidate must provide verification of a minimum of <u>five</u> years of education and/or architectural work experience to qualify for the ARE.

Candidates can satisfy the five-year requirement in a variety of ways:

- Provide verification of a professional degree in architecture through a program that is accredited by NAAB or CACB.

  OR

- Provide verification of at least five years of educational equivalents.

  OR

- Provide proof of work experience under the direct supervision of a licensed architect.

2. **How to qualify for an architect license**

Again, each jurisdiction has its own requirements. An individual typically needs a combination of about <u>eight</u> years of education and experience, as well as passing scores on the ARE exams. See the following link:
http://www.ncarb.org/Reg-Board-Requirements

For example, the requirements to become a licensed architect in California are:
- Eight years of post-secondary education and/or work experience as evaluated by the Board (including at least one year of work experience under the direct supervision of an architect licensed in a U.S. jurisdiction or two years of work experience under the direct supervision of an architect registered in a Canadian province)
- Completion of the Comprehensive Intern Development Program (CIDP) and the Intern Development Program (IDP)
- Successful completion of the Architect Registration Examinations (ARE)
- Successful completion of the California Supplemental Examination (CSE)

California does NOT require an accredited degree in architecture for examination and licensure. However, many other states do.

3. **What is the purpose of the ARE?**

The purpose of ARE is NOT to test a candidate's competency on every aspect of architectural practice. Its purpose is to test a candidate's competency on providing professional services to protect the <u>health, safety, and welfare</u> of the public. It tests candidates on the <u>fundamental</u> knowledge of pre-design, site design, building design, building systems, and construction documents and services.

The ARE tests a candidate's competency as a "specialist" on architectural subjects. It also tests her abilities as a "generalist" to coordinate other consultants' works.

You can download the exam content and references for each of the ARE divisions at the following link:
http://www.ncarb.org/are/40/StudyAids.html

4. **What is NCARB's rolling clock?**
   a. Starting on January 1, 2006, a candidate MUST pass ALL ARE sections within five years A passing score for an ARE division is only valid for five years, and a candidate must retake this division if he has NOT passed all divisions within the five year period.

   b. Starting on January 1, 2011, a candidate who is authorized to take the ARE MUST sit for at least one division of the exams within five years after receiving authorization. Otherwise, the candidate MUST reapply for authorization to test from an NCARB member board.

These rules were created in the **NCARB's rolling clock** resolution and passed by the NCARB council in the 2004 NCARB Annual Meeting.

5. **How to register for an ARE exam**
   Go to the following website and register:
   http://www.prometric.com/NCARB/default.htm

6. **How early do I need to arrive at the test center?**
   Be at the test center at least 30 minutes BEFORE your scheduled test time, OR you may lose your exam fee.

7. **Exam format &time**
   All ARE divisions are administered and graded by computer. Their detailed exam format and time allowances are as follows:

   1) **Programming, Planning & Practice (PPP)**
      The **Programming, Planning & Practice** division of the Architect Registration Exam (ARE) includes a multiple-choice (MC) section and a graphic vignette section, which lasts a total of 4 hours. The breakdown is:

Introduction Time:	15 minutes	
MC Testing Time:	**2 hours**	**85 items**
Scheduled Break:	15 minutes	
Introduction Time:	15 minutes	
Graphic Testing Time:	**1 hour**	**Site Zoning (1 vignette)**
Exit Questionnaire:	15 minutes	
Total Time	**4 hours**	

   2) **Site Planning & Design (SPD)**

Introduction Time:	15 minutes	
MC Testing Time:	**1.5 hours**	**65 items**
Scheduled Break:	15 minutes	
Introduction Time:	15 minutes	
2 Graphic Vignettes:	**2 hours**	**Site Grading, Site Design**
Exit Questionnaire:	15 minutes	
Total Time	**4.5 hours**	

   3) **Building Design & Construction Systems (BDCS)**

Introduction Time:	15 minutes	
MC Testing Time:	**1.75 hours**	**85 items**
Scheduled Break:	15 minutes	
Introduction Time:	15 minutes	
3 Graphic Vignettes:	**2.75 hours**	**Accessibility/Ramp, Stair Design, Roof Plan**
Exit Questionnaire:	15 minutes	
Total Time	**5.5 hours**	

4) Schematic Design (SD)

Introduction Time:	15 minutes	
Graphic Testing Time:	**1 hour**	**Interior Layout (1 vignette)**
Scheduled Break:	15 minutes	
Introduction Time:	15 minutes	
Graphic Testing Time:	**4 hours**	**Building Layout (1 vignette)**
Exit Questionnaire:	15 minutes	
Total Time	**6 hours**	

5) Structural Systems (SS)

Introduction Time:	15 minutes	
MC Testing Time:	**3.5 hours**	**125 items**
Scheduled Break:	15 minutes	
Introduction Time:	15 minutes	
Graphic Testing Time:	**1 hour**	**Structural Layout (1 vignette)**
Exit Questionnaire:	15 minutes	
Total Time	**5.5 hours**	

6) Building Systems (BS)

Introduction Time:	15 minutes	
MC Testing Time:	**2 hours**	**95 items**
Scheduled Break:	15 minutes	
Introduction Time:	15 minutes	
Graphic Testing Time:	**1 hour**	**Mechanical & Electrical Plan (1 vignette)**
Exit Questionnaire:	15 minutes	
Total Time	**4 hours**	

7) Construction Documents and Service (CDS)

Introduction Time:	15 minutes	
MC Testing Time:	**2 hours**	**100 items**
Scheduled Break:	15 minutes	
Introduction Time:	15 minutes	
Graphic Testing Time:	**1 hour**	**Building Section (1 vignette)**
Exit Questionnaire:	15 minutes	
Total Time	**4 hours**	

8. How are ARE scores reported?

All ARE scores are reported as Pass or Fail. ARE scores are usually processed within 4 to 6 weeks, and are then sent to your Board of Architecture. Your board then does additional processing and forwards the scores to you.

9. Is there a fixed percentage of candidates who pass the ARE exams?

No, there is NOT a fixed passing or failing percentage. If you meet the minimum competency required to practice as an architect, you pass. The passing scores are the same for all Boards of Architecture.

10. When can I retake a failed ARE division?

You can only take the same ARE division once within a 6-month period.

11. How much time do I need to prepare for each ARE division?

Every person is different, but on average you need about 40 hours to 80 hours for each ARE division. Set a realistic study schedule and stick with it. Make sure you allow time for personal and recreational commitments. If you are working full time, my suggestion is that you allow no less than 2 weeks but NOT more than 2 months to prepare for each ARE division. Do NOT drag out the exam prep process too long and risk losing your momentum.

12. Which ARE division should I take first?

This is a matter of personal preference, and you should make the final decision.

Some people like to start with the easier divisions and pass them first. This way, they build more confidence as they study and pass each division.

Other people like to start with the more difficult divisions so that if they fail, they can keep busy studying and taking the other divisions, while the clock is ticking. Before they know it six months has passed and they can reschedule if needed.

Programming, Planning & Practice (PPP) and Building Design & Construction Systems (BDCS) divisions often include some content from the Construction Documents and Service (CDS) division. It may be a good idea to start with CDS and then schedule the exams for PPP and BDCS soon after.

13. ARE exam prep and test-taking tips

You can start with Construction Documents and Service (CDS) and Structural Systems (SS) first because both divisions give a limited scope, and you may want to study building regulations and architectural history (especially famous architects and buildings that set the trends at critical turning points) before you take other divisions.

Complete mock exams and vignettes, including those provided by NCARB's practice program and this book, to hone your skills.

Form study groups and be familiar with the exam experience of other ARE candidates. The forum at our website is a helpful resource. See the following link: http://GreenExamEducation.com/

Take the ARE exams as soon as you become eligible, since you probably still remember portions of what you learned in architectural school, especially structural and architectural history. Do not make excuses for yourself and put off the exams.

The following test-taking tips may help you:

- Pace yourself properly. Spend about one minute for each Multiple-Choice (MC) question, except for the SS division questions, which you can spend about one and a half minutes on.
- Read the questions carefully and pay attention to words like *best, could, not, always, never, seldom, may, false, except,* etc.
- For questions that you are not sure of, eliminate the obvious wrong answer and then make an educated guess. Please note that if you do NOT answer the question, you automatically lose the point. If you guess, you at least have a chance to get it right.
- If you have no idea what the correct answer is and cannot eliminate any obvious wrong answers, then do not waste too much time on the question; just guess. Try to use the same guess answer for all of the questions you have no idea about. For example, if you choose "d" as the guess answer, then you should be consistent and use "d" whenever you have no clue. This way, you are likely to have a better chance at guessing more answers correctly.
- Mark the difficult questions, answer them, and come back to review them AFTER you finish all MC questions. If you are still not sure, go with your first choice. Your first choice is often the best.
- You really need to spend time practicing to become VERY familiar with NCARB's graphic software and know every command well. This is because the ARE graphic vignette is a timed test, and you do NOT have time to think about how to use the NCARB graphic software during the test. If you do not know how, you will NOT be able to finish your solution on time.
- The ARE exams test a candidate's competency to provide professional services protecting the <u>health, safety, and welfare</u> of the public. Do NOT waste time on aesthetic or other design elements not required by the program.

ARE exams are difficult, but if you study hard and prepare well, combined with your experience, IDP training, and/or college education, you should be able to pass all divisions and eventually be able to call yourself an architect.

14. English system (English or inch-pound units) versus metric system (SI units)

This book is based on the English system or English units; the equivalent value in metric system or SI units follows in parentheses. All SI dimensions are in millimeters unless noted otherwise. The English or inch-pound units are based on the module used in the U.S. The SI units noted are simple conversions from the English units for information only and are not necessarily according to a metric module.

15. Codes and standards used in this book

We use the following codes and standards:

American Institute of Architects, Contract Documents, Washington, DC.

Canadian Construction Documents Committee, CCDC Standard Documents, 2006, Ottawa.

16. Where can I find study materials on architectural history?

Every ARE exam may have a few questions related to architectural history. The following are some helpful links to FREE study materials on the topic:

http://issuu.com/motimar/docs/history_synopsis?viewMode=magazine
http://www.ironwarrior.org/ARE/Materials_Methods/m_m_notes_2.pdf

Chapter Two

Building Systems (BS) Division

A. General Information

1. Exam content

An architect should be able to evaluate, select, coordinate, and integrate the mechanical, electrical, plumbing, and specialty systems during building design and construction.

The exam content for the BS division of the ARE includes:
1) Codes &Regulations (5% to 8%)
2) Environmental Issues (10% to 15%)
3) Plumbing: Principles and Materials &Technology (10% to 15%)
4) Heating, Ventilating, and Air-Conditioning Systems (HVAC): Principles and Materials &Technology (18% to 23%)
5) Electrical: Principles and Materials & Technology (10% to 15%)
6) Lighting: Principles and Materials & Technology (18% to 23%)
7) Specialties: Acoustics, Communications & Security, Conveying Systems, and Fire Detection &Suppression (14% to 19%)

For the graphic vignette, you will be required to draw a reflected ceiling plan that incorporates structural, mechanical, and lighting systems, as well as life safety concerns.

2. Official exam guide and practice program for the BS division

Read the official exam guide for the BS division at least twice. Make sure you install the BS division practice program on your computer and become very familiar with it. The real exam is VERY similar to the practice example.

B. Important Documents and Publications for BS Division of the ARE exam

The BS division covers a broad range of material. You may also have a few questions from other divisions, such as CDS and BDCS.

Based on our research, the most important documents/publications for BS division of the ARE exam are as follows:

1. NCARB Building Systems division list of references and formulas (BSreferences.pdf)

This a free PDF file available at the NCARB website. See the following link:
http://www.ncarb.org/en/ARE/Preparing-for-the-ARE.aspx

In the real BS exam, you can expect about **20 questions with calculations** in the MC portion. These questions are NOT too difficult and are based on the NCARB Building Systems division list of references and formulas sheet found at the link above. Read this MANY times to make sure you understand and are VERY familiar with all of the formulas. This reference sheet will be available during the test, but you do NOT want to waste valuable time during the exam learning how.

FYI: NCARB made an error on the second electrical formula on the reference sheet.

The bottom formula on the reference sheet will make sense if the (lumens) is changed to **(lumens per fixture)**, which = (lumens per lamp) x (number of lamps per fixture).

You need to know that **luminaires** means fixtures.

So the second electrical formula on the reference sheet should correctly read:

Number of luminaires = (footcandles) x (floor area) / (lumens per fixture) x (CU) x (LLF), where CU = coefficient of utilization and LLF = Light Lost Factor

Note: In the ARE exams, it may be a good idea to skip any calculation question that requires over 30 seconds of your time; just pick a guess answer, mark it, and come back to calculate it at the end. This way, you have more time to read and answer other easier questions correctly.

A calculation question that takes 20 minutes to answer will gain the same number of points as a simple question that ONLY takes 2 minutes.

If you spend 20 minutes on a calculation question earlier, you risk losing the time to read and answer ten other easier questions, which could result in a loss of ten points instead of one.

2. ***Mechanical and Electrical Equipment for Buildings* (MEEB)**
Walter T. Grondzik, Alison G. Kwok, Benjamin Stein, and John S. Reynolds. *Mechanical and Electrical Equipment for Buildings* (MEEB). Wiley, latest edition (The latest edition is the 11th edition.)This is a huge but useful book with 1,792 pages.

Expect about 60% to 70% of the MC questions in BS division to be based on content from this book.

Many of the diagrams for the sample questions in the official NCARB Exam Guide come directly out of MEEB, such as vibration isolator (sample question 33).

Do NOT let this huge book overwhelm you. Do NOT spend too much time on MEEB. Do NOT get carried away by the tiny details and do NOT try to memorize **everything**. Just read or look through the book several times and memorize only the things you **are required to memorize**.

Focus on the **most important items** of the book. Study all the **images, diagrams, and charts**, and read the related paragraphs if you find a diagram or chart confusing. This can be a good way to deal with a huge book like this. **Read the important items several times** in order to retain this information.

Note: Your time and effort are the most important assets for any exam prep. Cherish these items and only focus on the most important information. Do NOT spread yourself too thin.

*Do NOT even think about reading MEEB line by line or from cover to cover. This will consume too much of your time, and you may NOT gain anything from the exercise. Instead, skim through it a few times, jump back and forth if you need to, and focus on the portions that you do not know or are unfamiliar with. Try to take as much **critical** information as possible from the book WITHOUT reading it line by line or from cover to cover. Focus on the **images, diagrams, and charts**.*

Remember your goal is NOT to read MEEB line by line or from cover to cover; your goal is to prepare and pass the BS division with LIMITED time and effort.

The following is a link to the **MEEB online quizzes**:
http://bcs.wiley.com/he-bcs/Books?action=resource&bcsId=2879&itemId=0471465917&resourceId=7094

Note: Complete ALL of the MEEB online quizzes at least once and make sure you understand ALL of the answers. These quizzes will only take you a few hours total.

3. ***Architectural Graphic Standards (AGS)***
   Ramsey, Charles George, and John Ray Hoke Jr. *Architectural Graphic Standards.* The American Institute of Architects & Wiley, latest edition.

   There may be a few questions asking you to identify some basic graphic symbols. Expect **many** diagrams similar to those shown in AGS to show up in the real ARE BS division exam. This is a good book to skim through, focusing on the portions related to the BS divisions, like mechanical, electrical, plumbing, and fire protection sections. The **images, diagrams, and charts are especially useful**.

   Many of the diagrams for the sample questions in the official NCARB Exam Guide come directly from AGS, such as valve types and their uses (sample question 14),and the diagram for a typical chiller and cooling tower cycle (sample question 15).

4. ***ADAAG Manual: A Guide to the American with Disabilities Accessibility Guidelines***
   Access Board, *ADAAG Manual: A Guide to the American with Disabilities Accessibility Guidelines.* East Providence, RI: BNI Building News.
   ADA Standards for Accessible Design are available as FREE PDF files at:
   http://www.ada.gov/

AND
http://www.access-board.gov/adaag/html/figures/index.html

There may be a few questions pertaining to ADA on the exam.

5. ***Building Construction Illustrated (BCI)***
Ching, D. K. and Cassandra Adams. *Building Construction Illustrated.* John Wiley & Sons, latest edition.

Read the sections related to the BS division. Pay attention to images, diagrams, and charts.

6. ***International Building Code (IBC)***
International Code Council, Inc. (ICC, 2006), *International Building Code* (IBC).You may have a few questions based on this publication. Become familiar with some of the commonly used code sections, such as allowable areas and allowable areas increase, unlimited areas, egresses, width and numbers of exits required, minimum exit passage width, occupancy groups and related exit occupancy load factors, types of construction, minimum number of required plumbing fixtures required, etc.

See the following link for some FREE IBC code sections citations:
http://publiccodes.citation.com/icod/ibc/2006f2/index.htm?bu=IC-P-2006-000001&bu2=IC-P-2006-000019

See the appendix of this book for other official reference materials suggested by NCARB.

7. **Construction Specifications Institute (CSI) MasterFormat &** ***Building Construction***
Become familiar with the new 6-digit CSI Construction Specifications Institute (CSI) MasterFormat as there may be a few questions based on this publication. Make sure you know which items/materials belong to which CSI MasterFormat specification section, and memorize the major sections names and related numbers. For example, Division 9 is Finishes, and Division 5 is Metal, etc. Another one of my books, *Building Construction*, has detailed discussions on CSI MasterFormat specification sections.

Mnemonics for the 2004 CSI Master Format

The following is a good mnemonic, which relates to the2004 CSI Master Format division names. Bold font signals the gaps in the numbering sequence.

This tool can save you lots of time: if you can remember the four sentences below, you can easily memorize the order of the 2004 CSI Master Format divisions. The number sequencing is a bit more difficult, but can be mastered if you remember the five bold words and numbers that are not sequential. Memorizing this material will not only help you in several divisions of the ARE, but also in real architectural practice

Mnemonics (pay attention to the underlined letters):
Good students can memorize material when teachers order.

F students earn F's simply 'cause **forgetting** principles have **an** effect. (21 and 25)
C students **end** everyday understanding things without memorizing. (31)
Please make professional pollution prevention inventions **everyday**. (40 and 48)

1-Good..............................General Requirements
2-Students.........................(Site) now Existing Conditions
3-Can...............................Concrete
4-Memorize.........................Masonry
5-Material ....Metals
6-When.............................Woods and Plastics
7-Teachers.........................Thermal and Moisture
8-Order.............................Openings

9-F..................................Finishes
10-Students........................Specialties
11-Earn.............................Equipment
12-F's..............................Furnishings
13-Simply..........................Special Construction
14-'Cause..........................Conveying
21-Forgetting ....**Fire**
22-Principles......................Plumbing
23-Have............................HVAC
25-An..............................**Automation**
26-Effect..........................Electric

27-C................................Communication
28-Students........................Safety & Security
31-End.............................**Earthwork**
32-Everyday........................Exterior
33-Understanding ....Utilities
34-Things..........................Transportation
35-Without Memorizing.......Waterways and Marine

40-Please.........................**Process Integration**
41-Make............................Material Processing and Handling Equipment
42-Professional...................Process Heating, Cooling, and Drying Equipment
43-Pollution.......................Process Gas and Liquid Handling, Purification and Storage
                                        Equipment
44-Prevention....................Pollution Control Equipment
45-Inventions.....................Industry-Specific Manufacturing Equipment
48-Everyday.....................**Electrical Power Generation**

Note:
There are 49 CSI divisions. The "missing" divisions are those "reserved for future expansion" by CSI. They are intentionally omitted from the list.

C. Strategies, Tips, a Step-by Step Solution, and Notes on NCARB Traps

1. Overall strategies

To most candidates, the Multiple Choice (MC) portions are harder than the graphic vignettes. Some of the MC questions are based on experience and there is NOT really a set of fixed study materials for them. You WILL make some mistakes on the MC questions no matter how hard you study.

On the other hand, the graphic vignettes are relatively easier, and you can prepare for them in a short time to improve your score substantially. Try to **nail all the graphic vignettes** perfectly. This way, you will have a much better chance to pass the exam even if you answer some MC questions incorrectly.

Tips: *Many people do poorly on the MC portion of the BS division, especially those who do NOT have a lot of working experience, but curiously, not too many people fail the exam because of the MC portion. Most people fail the ENTIRE BS section because they have made **one** fatal mistake on the graphic vignette section, such as showing a rigid duct running **perpendicular** to joists more than two feet from a steel beam or bearing wall. So, practice the NCARB BS practice program graphic software fastidiously and make sure you absolute NAIL the vignettes section. This is key for you to pass.*

The official NCARB BS exam guide gives a passing and failing solution to each of the sample vignettes, but it does NOT show you the step-by-step details.

I am going to fill in the blanks here and offer you these instructions, command by command.

You really need to spend time practicing to become VERY familiar with NCARB's graphic software. This is because ARE graphic vignettes are timed, and you do NOT have the luxury to think about how to use the software during the exam. Otherwise, you may NOT be able to finish your solution on time.

The following solution is based on the official NCARB BS practice program for the **ARE4.0**. Future versions of ARE may have some minor changes, but the principles and fundamental elements should be the same. The official NCARB BS practice program has not changed much since its introduction, and the earlier versions are VERY similar to, or the same as, the current ARE 4.0. The actual graphic vignette of the BS division should be VERY, VERY similar to the practice one on NCARB's website.

2. Tips for the graphic vignette section

1) Install the NCARB BS practice program, and become familiar with it. I am NOT going to repeat the vignette description and requirements here since they are already written out in the NCARB practice program.

   See the following link for a FREE download of the NCARB practice program:
   http://www.ncarb.org/ARE/Preparing-for-the-ARE.aspx

2) Review the general test directions, vignette directions, program, and tips carefully.
3) Press the space bar to go to the work screen.
4) Read the program and codes in the NCARB Exam Guide several times the week before your exam. Become VERY familiar with this material, and you will be able to read the problem requirements MUCH faster during the real exam because you can immediately identify which criteria are different from the practice exam.

3. A Step-by-step solution to the official NCARB practice program graphic vignette: Mechanical & Electrical Plan

1) Determine the **spacing for the recessed fluorescent fixtures:**
   - The vertical distance between the desk level and ceiling = the ceiling height – the desk height = 9'-0" – 3'-0"= 6'-0".
   - The required light level is approximately 50 footcandles measured at desk level.
   - For both the **sides** and **ends of the 2'x2' lights** and the short **ends** of the 2'x4' lights, use the appropriate lighting diagram to determine the spacing. In the fluorescent fixture 2'x2' and 2'x4' (end) diagrams, the line at 6'-0" below the ceiling intersects the curved line representing 50 footcandles at 2'-0" from the edge of the recessed fluorescent fixture. This means we need to place 2'x2' lights and the short **ends** of the 2'x4' lights approximately 2'-0" from the walls and 4'-0" apart from one another.
   - For the long **sides** of the 2'x4' lights use the lighting diagram with the subtitle "Recessed Fluorescent Fixture 2'x4' Side."Here we notice the line 6'-0" below the ceiling intersects the curved line representing 50 footcandles at 3'-0" from the edge of the recessed fluorescent fixture. This means we need to place the long **sides** of the 2'x4' lights 3'-0" from the walls and 6'-0" apart from one another.

*Note: It is **absolute critical** for ARE candidates to learn how **to read the lighting diagrams**. This is key to passing the ARE BS division vignette. For the lighting diagrams in the NCARB practice program, the numbers on the left side show the vertical distance from the ceiling; the numbers along the bottom line represent the horizontal distance from the edge of the light fixture; and the curvilinear lines mark the lighting level in footcandles.*

It is almost impossible to get the EXACT 50 footcandles in each room as required by the NCARB program. Every room will be over or under lit. Get as close to 50 footcandles as you can, and evenly light each space.

2) Use **Draw > Grid and** click on two opposite corners of the Reception/Secretary Room to draw the grid (figure 2.1). Keep the following in mind when laying out the ceiling grid:

- Make the ceiling grid symmetrical in order to provide an even lighting level within the room.
- The layout should be oriented with respect to the lights and spacing we discovered in previous steps.

3) **Adjust** the ceiling grid to make it look symmetrical:

- Use the **move, adjust** tool and click anywhere within the grid rectangle to shift the cells within.
- Use the **move, adjust** tool and click on an edge of the grid rectangle to increase or decrease the length or width of the entire object (figure 2.2).

4) Use **Draw > Recessed Fluorescent Fixture – 2'x2'x6"** to draw four lights and place them approximately 2'-0" from the walls and 4'-0" apart from one another (figure 2.3).

5) Find the square footage of the grid, which is also the square footage of the Reception/Secretary Room:

- Click on **id?** and then click anywhere within the grid. On the lower left hand corner of the screen, you will see **Grid: 169 ft²** (figure 2.4).

  Note*: This is an important trick to avoid calculating the room area manually and will save your time in the real exam*

- Since the program states you need to provide one supply diffuser and one return-air grille for every 144 s.f. of floor area (or portion thereof), in the Reception/Secretary Room. We will show two supply diffusers and two return-air grilles because169/144 = 1.17.

6) Use **Draw > Diffuser** to draw two supply diffusers and spread them evenly throughout the room (figure 2.5).

7) Use **Draw > Return-Air Grille** to draw two return-air grilles, and spread them evenly. Separate the diffusers and return-air grilles as much as you can. They should be at least 4'-0"apart (figure 2.6).

8) Click on **rotate** to turn each return-air grille 90 degrees, and then use **move, adjust** to place the return-air grilles so that each one is supported by the grid on three sides (figure 2.7).

Note: It is best to have the diffusers and return-air grilles supported by the grid on three sides.

OR

Place the two short edges of the return-air grilles on the grid, and align the long edge along the side of a 2'x2' recessed fluorescent fixture. This is useful for some difficult conditions. In this case, the grid on the two short edges supports the return-air grille. The fluorescent fixture is NOT acting as a support.

The NCARB program NEVER explicitly states *that you HAVE to have the diffusers and return-air grilles supported by the grid on three sides, but it is good practice.*

If you place one short edge of the return-air grille on the grid, and another short edge on a fluorescent fixture (figure 2.6), this is another story and is NOT acceptable, because you are using a fluorescent fixture as a supporting point.

9) Repeat the previous steps to draw the grid, supply diffusers, return-air grilles, and lights for the remaining rooms.

10) Click **rotate** and then click anywhere within the grid to modify the orientation of the grid (figure 2.8).In this particular problem, we also have made a minor adjustment to the lighting placement of the Files Room/Sample Room so that the lighting level is spread more evenly than the NCARB sample solution shows.

11) Use **Draw > Rigid Duct** to draw the rigid ducts for the supply and return air. Do NOT forget the short rigid duct for the return air (figure 2.9).

   *Note: Rigid ducts that run **perpendicular** to joists must be within 2'-0" of a steel beam or bearing wall.*

12) Use **Draw > Fire Damper** to draw the fire damper. Click on **rotate** and then the fire damper symbol. Turn it so that the short "leg" points **in the direction of air travel** inside the duct (figure 2.10).

13) Use **Draw > Flexible Duct** to connect the flexible ducts to ALL diffusers, even if they overlap or touch the rigid duct. Do NOT miss any diffusers. Flexible duct lengths should not exceed 10'-0" (figure 2.11). When you draw a flexible duct, its length is displayed on the lower left corner of the screen.

   Note: A single flex duct can only connect one supply diffuser. Do NOT use it to connect more than one.

14) Determine the **spacing for the accent light fixtures** in the Architect's office:
   - For accent light fixtures, the NCARB program requires the light level **between** the fixtures at 5'-0"**above** the floor (or 4'-0" from the ceiling) to be 80 footcandles.
   - Using the lighting diagrams for accent light fixtures, we notice that the line 4'-0" below the ceiling intersects the curved line representing 80 footcandles at 2'-0" from the edge of the fixture.

Note: Accent lights focus on the wall (a vertical surface), NOT the desk (a horizontal surface). The requirement in the program is for 80 footcandles ON the wall BETWEEN fixtures. So you can use 4'-0" diameter sketch circles to assist you in locating the accent lights; they should intersect AT the wall.

15) Use **zoom** to enlarge in the Architect's office, and then **Sketch > Circle** to draw some circles with 2'-0" radiuses to assist you in locating the accent light fixtures. The circles should **intersect** AT the west wall. The centers of the circles will inform the locations of the accent light fixtures (figure 2.12).

*Note: For each the accent light fixture at 5'-0"**above** the floor (or 4'-0" from the ceiling), the lighting level is 80 footcandles at the circle perimeter, lower than 80 footcandles outside the circle, and higher than 80 footcandles inside the circle.*

16) Because the accent light fixtures are **recessed**, they can NOT overlap the ceiling grid, fluorescent fixtures, supply diffusers, or return-air grilles. You may have to make some adjustment to allow for the recessed accent fixtures:
   - Use **move group** to move the grid, supply diffusers, and return-air grilles to the right.
   - Click on **move, adjust** and then on an **edge** of the grid rectangle to align it with the west wall. Use the same procedure to adjust the grid to the east wall. Then adjust the ends of the flexible ducts to match them with the new locations of the supply diffusers (figure 2.13).

Note: Of course, you can draw the circles first and then draw the remaining items to avoid the trouble of moving and adjusting all the elements in the room.

*The previous steps are very good exercise for you to practice the **move group** and **move, adjust** tools just in case you do need to use them in the real exam. The above steps show you some tips on using these tools.*

17) Use **Draw > Recessed Accent Fixture** to draw four accent light fixtures at the center of each circle (figure 2.14).

Note: The accent light fixtures are very small, and people tend to miss them. Make sure you remember to draw them.

18) Use **zoom** to show the entire floor plan and click **Sketch > Hide Sketch Elements** to hide any construction lines created with the sketch tool. Your final solution will look like figure 2.15.

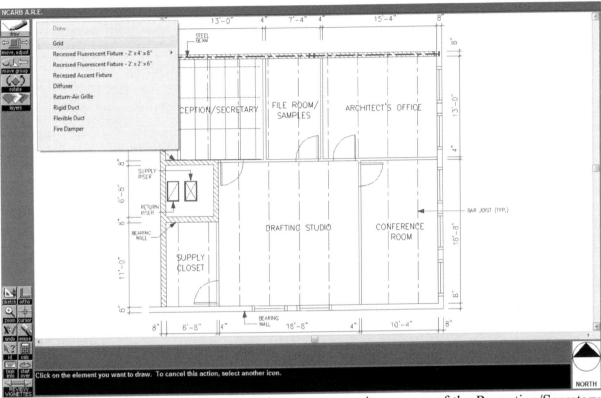

Figure 2.1   Use **Draw > Grid and** click on two opposite corners of the Reception/Secretary Room to draw the ceiling grid.

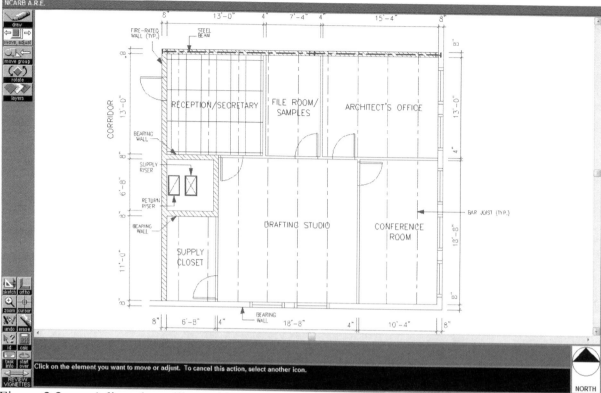

Figure 2.2   Adjust the ceiling grid to make it look symmetrical.

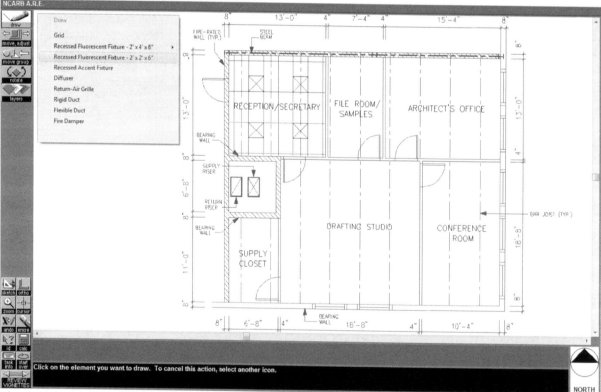

Figure 2.3   Use **Draw > Recessed Fluorescent Fixture – 2'x2'x6"** to draw four lights and place them approximately 2'-0" from the walls and 4'-0" apart.

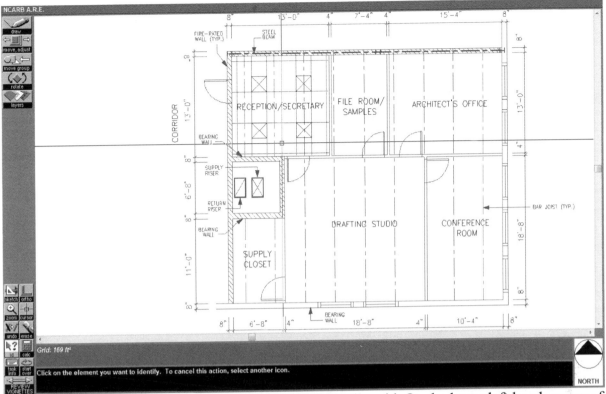

Figure 2.4   Click on **id?** then click anywhere within the grid. On the lower left hand corner of the screen, you will see **Grid: 169 ft²**.

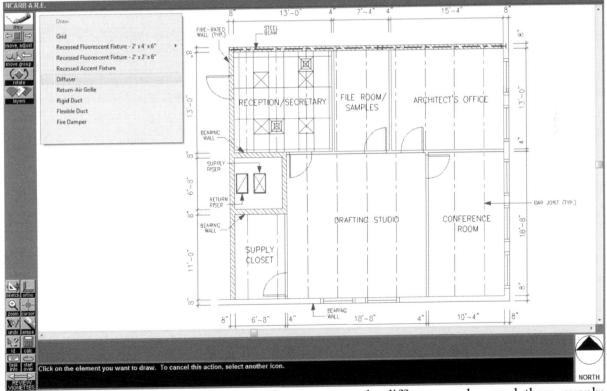

Figure 2.5   Use **Draw > Diffuser** to draw two supply diffusers, and spread them evenly throughout the room.

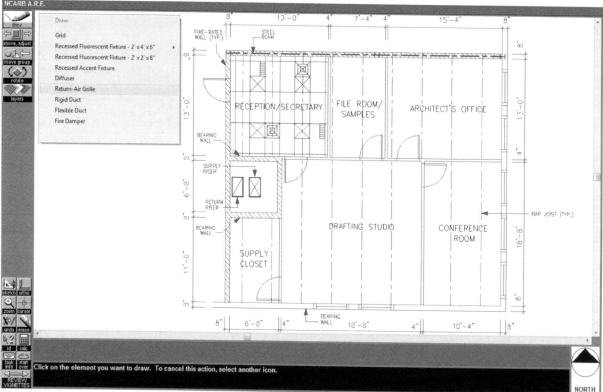

Figure 2.6   Use **Draw > Return Air Grille** to draw two return-air grilles, and spread them evenly throughout the room.

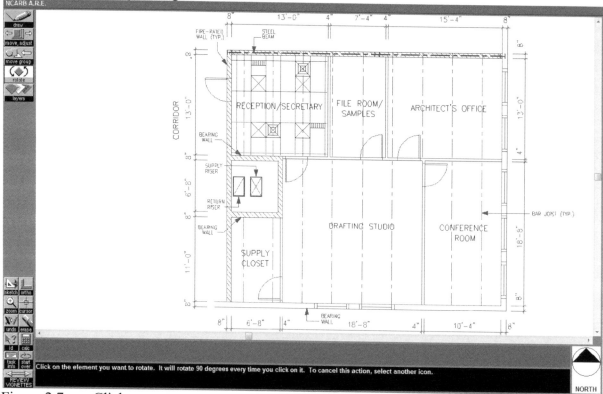

Figure 2.7   Click on **rotate** to turn each return-air grille 90 degrees, and then use **move, adjust** to position each one.

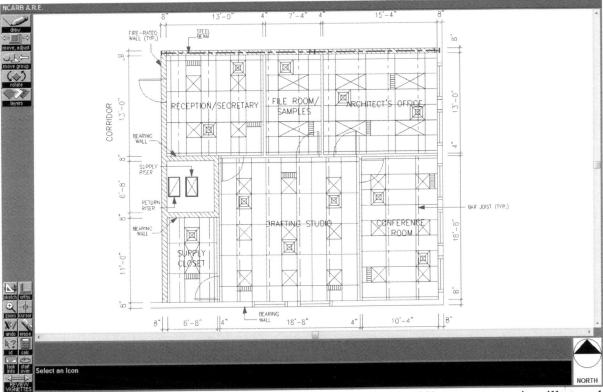

Figure 2.8   Repeat the previous steps and draw the grid, supply diffusers, return-air grilles, and lights for the remaining rooms.

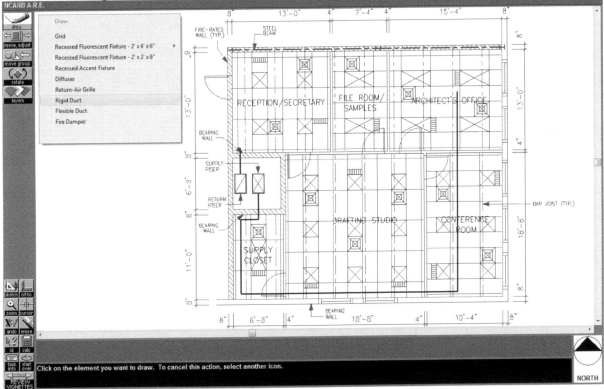

Figure 2.9   Use **Draw > Rigid Duct** to draw the supply and return air duct.

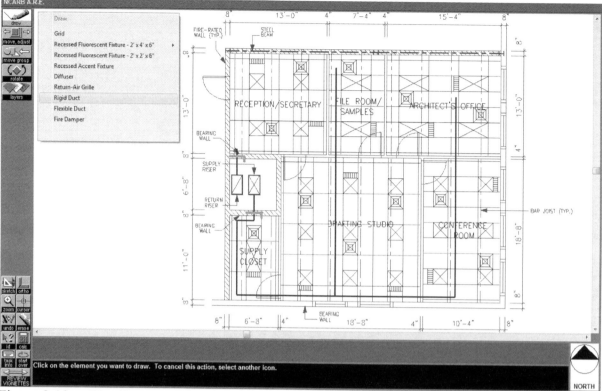

Figure 2.10   Use **Draw > Fire Damper** to draw the fire damper. Click on **rotate** to turn the symbol.

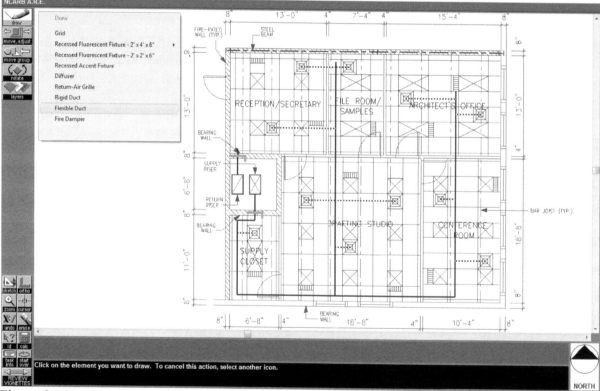

Figure 2.11   Use **Draw > Flexible Duct** to draw the flexible ducts to ALL diffusers, even if they overlap or touch the rigid duct.

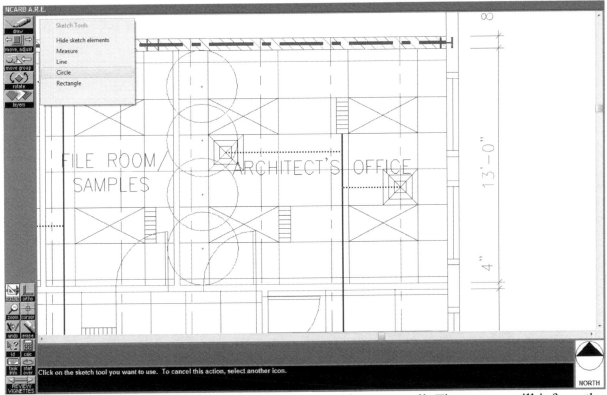

Figure 2.12   The sketch circles should **intersect** AT the west wall. The centers will inform the locations of the accent light fixtures.

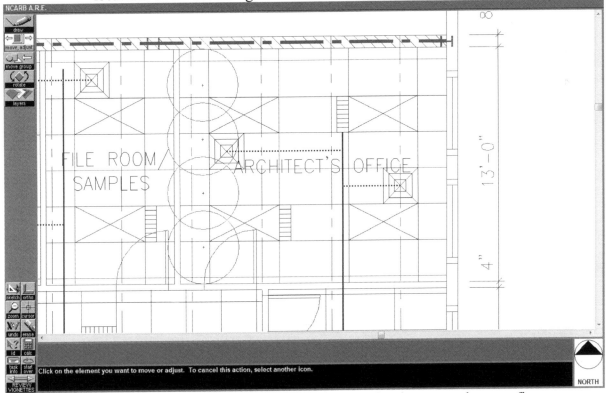

Figure 2.13   You may have to make adjustments to allow for the recessed accent fixtures.

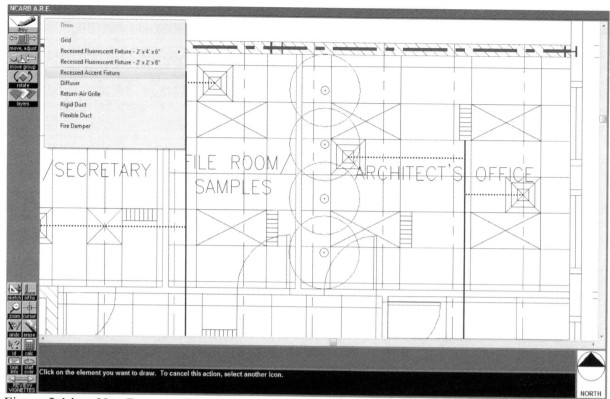

Figure 2.14   Use **Draw > Recessed Accent Fixture** to draw four accent light fixtures at the center of each sketch circle.

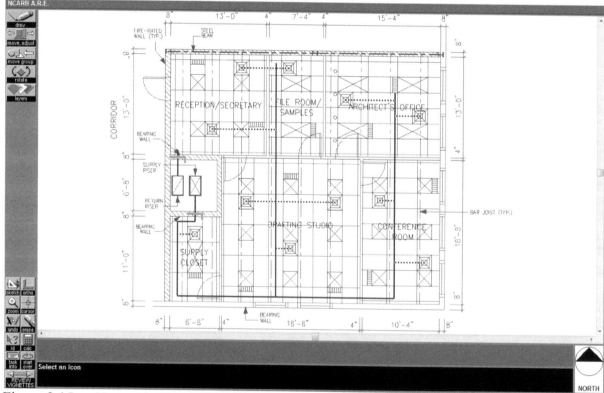

Figure 2.15   Use **zoom** to see the entire floor plan. Use **Sketch> Hide Sketch Elements** to hide sketch elements. This is your final solution.

4. **Notes on NCARB traps**

Pay attention to the following to avoid falling into a NCARB trap:

- The ceiling space serves as a return-air plenum. Do NOT forget to connect the return-air plenum to the return riser with **a rigid duct and a fire damper**.
- Use the "rotate" tool to properly orient all fire dampers: The short "leg" of the fire damper symbol should point **in the direction of air travel** inside the duct.
- Rigid ducts do **not** fit through joists or in the area between the bottom of joists and ceiling.
- Rigid ducts fit under beams and in spaces between joists.
  Note: This requirement is different from the ARE CDS division vignette.
- Rigid ducts that run **perpendicular** to joists must be within 2'-0" of a beam or bearing wall.
- Connect each supply diffuser to the rigid supply duct system with a flexible duct, even when the diffuser is right under the rigid supply duct.
- Draw flexible ducts to ALL diffusers, even if they overlap or touch the rigid duct.
- Flexible duct lengths shall not exceed 10'-0".
- Flexible ducts fit through joist webs.
- A flex duct can only connect one supply diffuser. Do NOT use it to connect more than one.
- Provide maximum flexibility for furniture layouts.
- Provide as much separation between the supply air diffusers and return air grille as possible.
- Provide one supply diffuser and one return-air grille for every 144 s.f. of floor area (or portion thereof) in each space.
- Do NOT waste time calculating square footages for each room when you try to layout the diffusers and return-air grilles. Draw the grid in the room first, and then click **id?** on the command palette. The software will give you this number.

Chapter Three

ARE Mock Exam for
Building Systems (BS) Division

A. Mock Exam: BS Multiple-Choice (MC) Section

1. An architect is designing an office with 1,500 s.f. (139.35 s.m.) of gross area. The owner's design criteria require 10,000 BTU per 300 s.f. of gross area (293.071 W per 27.87 s.m.). If the market price of a central air-conditioning system is $1,000 per ton and the system is only available in an integer ton, what is the minimum cost of a system for the office that will meet the owner's criteria?
   _____ dollars

2. You are designing a sewer line. The city requires a minimum slope of 1/4" per foot (2.08%) for sewer lines. If the sewer line has to run a horizontal distance of 90 feet (27.43m), the minimum vertical rise has to be_____ feet.

3. The transfer of heat from one place to another by the movement of fluids is called
   a. convection
   b. radiation
   c. conduction
   d. mass transfer

4. In plumbing, the unobstructed space between a wall mounted faucet and the sink rim is **(Check the two that apply.)**
   a. siphonage
   b. an air gap
   c. a form of backflow prevention
   d. a handicap clearance

5. A diagram that illustrates the relationships between dry bulb temperature, wet bulb temperature, and relative humidity, as well as other properties is called
   a. a dry bulb temperature chart
   b. a wet bulb temperature chart
   c. a human comfort factors chart
   d. a psychrometric chart

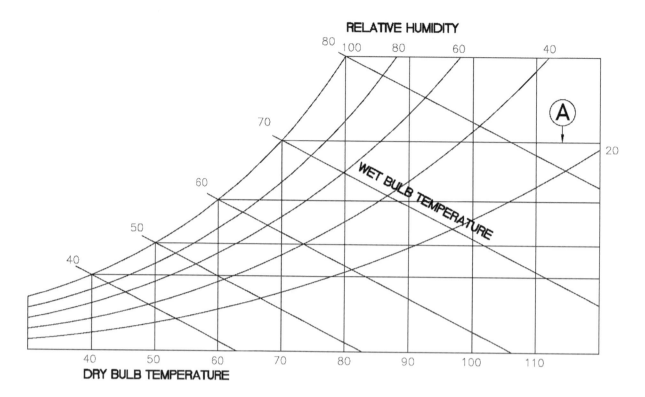

Figure 3.1   **Chart** (The temperatures are shown in °F, and the relative humidity is shown in percentages.)

6. The line labeled as "A" in figure 3.1 represents_____.

7. Per the *ADAAG Manual: A Guide to the American with Disabilities Accessibility Guidelines*, the operable parts that are essential to the basic operation of a telephone for a side reach approach can be a maximum of how many inches above the floor?
   a. 36"
   b. 48"
   c. 54"
   d. 60"

8. Which of the following statements regarding an electrical single line diagram are not true? **Check the two that apply.**
   a. Elements on the diagram represent the physical size or location of the electrical equipment.
   b. Elements on the diagram do not represent the physical size or location of the electrical equipment.
   c. Common convention dictates organization of the diagram with the same left-to-right, top-to-bottom sequence as the switchgear or other apparatus represented.
   d. Common convention does not dictate organization of the diagram with the same left-to-right, top-to-bottom sequence as the switchgear or other apparatus represented.

9. Which of the following are ways for the human body to lose heat? **Check the four that apply.**
   a. ventilation
   b. evaporation
   c. conduction
   d. convection
   e. radiation
   f. condensation

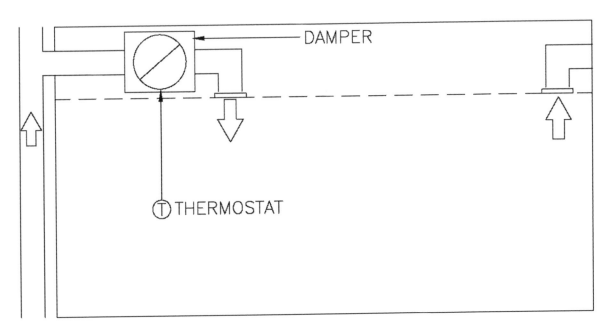

Figure 3.2   Air-Conditioning Distribution System

10. What type of air-conditioning distribution system is shown in figure 3.2?
    a. a single zone system
    b. a variable flow system
    c. a double duct system
    d. a terminal reheat system

11. Which of the following statements regarding air-conditioning units are not true? **Check the two that apply.**
    a. Packaged air-conditioning units are electrically powered heating and cooling units.
    b. Heat pumps are electrically powered heating and cooling units.
    c. Outdoor condensing units provide cooling for packaged air-conditioning units.
    d. Outdoor condensing units provide cooling for heat pumps.

12. _____ is a pressure surge that can occur when water is shut off or forced to change direction abruptly.

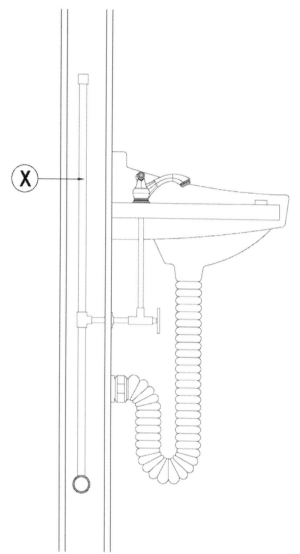

Figure 3.3   Plumbing Drawing

13. What is the term for X in figure 3.3?
    a. exhaust vent
    b. manufactured shock absorber
    c. capped air chamber
    d. vent pipe

14. Which of the following is a proper arrangement of building elements in a cold climate?
    a. For an exterior wall, from outside to inside: plaster, plywood, batt insulation, vapor barrier, water pipe, drywall
    b. For an exterior wall, from outside to inside: plaster, plywood, vapor barrier, batt insulation, water pipe, drywall
    c. For an exterior wall, from outside to inside: plaster, plywood, water pipe, batt insulation, vapor barrier, drywall
    d. For an exterior wall, from outside to inside: plaster, plywood, vapor barrier, water pipe, batt insulation, drywall

15. Which of the following statements are true? **Check the two that apply.**
    a. Both the roof drains and over flow drains should be connected to a storm drain if possible.
    b. Roof drains should be connected to a storm drain if possible.
    c. A floor drain can be connected to a sewer line.
    d. A grease interceptor can be connected to a sewer line.

16. Which of the following is graywater? **Check the two that apply.**
    a. rainwater
    b. water from dishwashers or kitchen sinks
    c. water from laundry tubs and clothes washers
    d. water from toilets

17. A pipe with a maximum of_____inch outside diameter can fit inside a 6" wood stud wall.

18. A 2" copper pipe means
    a. the inner diameter of the pipe is 2"
    b. the outside diameter of the pipe is 2"
    c. the inner diameter of the pipe is a little larger than 2"
    d. the inner diameter of the pipe is a little smaller than 2"

19. Receptacles in wet locations should be protected by a _____.

Figure 3.4   Electrical Plan Symbol

20. What does the electrical symbol in figure 3.4 represent?
    a. GFI
    b. GBFI
    c. grounded neutral
    d. generator

21. For a roof space accessible by the public or building tenants, what is the minimum height of a vent pipe extension?
    a. 6" above the roof
    b. 8" above the roof
    c. 6'-8"above the roof
    d. 7'-0"above the roof

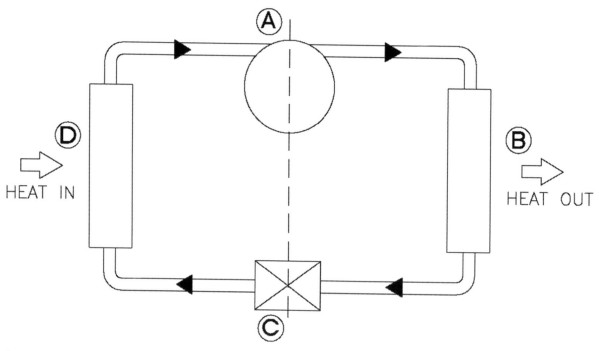

Figure 3.5   Refrigeration Flow Diagram

22. In the refrigeration flow diagram of figure 3.5, where is expansion valve located?
    a. A
    b. B
    c. C
    d. D

23. For a faucet in a house, what type of valve is most likely used?
    a. gate valve
    b. globe valve
    c. check valve
    d. angle valve

24. Which of the following may be a source of a building's heat gain? **Check the two that apply.**
    a. occupants
    b. lightning
    c. air infiltration
    d. insulation

25. Which of the following power supplies is common for residences?
    a. 120/240 V, single-phase, three-wire system
    b. 120/208 V, three-phase, four-wire system
    c. 277/480 V, three-phase, four-wire system
    d. 2400/4160 V, three-phase, four-wire system

26. Which of the following fixture types are permitted to connect to a soil stack vent? **Check the two that apply.**
    a. bidets
    b. urinals
    c. lavatories
    d. toilets

27. Underground water lines should be placed
    a. above the frost line
    b. with the centerline align with the frost line
    c. below the frost line
    d. none of the above

28. What is the minimum height of a handicapped accessible receptacle outlet above the floor?
    a. 6"
    b. 12"
    c. 15"
    d. 18"

29. Which piping material has the lowest coefficient of thermal expansion?
    a. PVC
    b. copper
    c. iron
    d. glass

30. The solar altitude is largest in the Northern Hemisphere on the day of the
    a. vernal equinox
    b. summer solstice
    c. autumnal equinox
    d. winter solstice

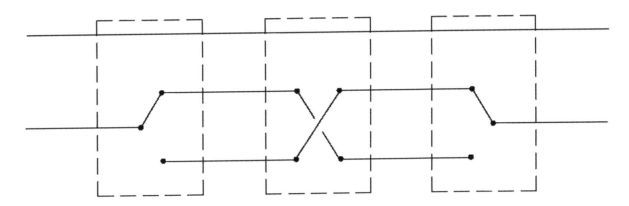

Figure 3.6   Switch Wiring Diagram

31. Which of the following devices control lighting from three different locations as indicated in Figure 3.6? **Check the two that apply.**
    a. two single-pole, single-throw switches
    b. two single-pole, double-throw switches
    c. one four-way switch
    d. one three-pole, double-throw switch

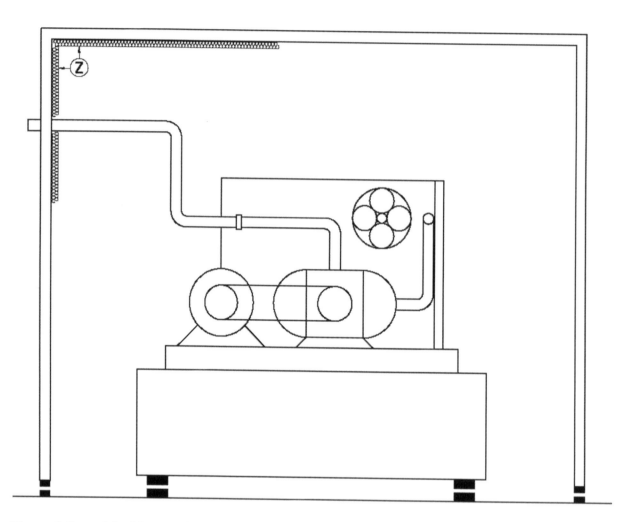

Figure 3.7   Machines and Appliances

32. What is the term for Z in figure 3.7?
    a. resilient hanger
    b. acoustical lining
    c. paver pedestal
    d. vibration isolator

33. Which of the following are not effective ways of controlling noise between two adjacent apartment units? **Check the two that apply.**
    a. flexible boots
    b. resilient hangers
    c. acoustical lining outside of the HVAC ducts
    d. acoustical lining inside of the HVAC ducts
    e. using stainless steel ducts

34. Which of the following statements are true? **Check the two that apply.**
    a. Duct silencers and baffles are normally placed inside the HVAC ducts.
    b. Duct silencers and baffles are normally placed outside the HVAC ducts.
    c. Duct silencers and baffles are useful to reduce fan noise but cause considerable pressure drop.
    d. Duct silencers and baffles are not useful to reduce fan noise and cause considerable pressure drop.

35. Which of the following statements regarding fixture installation and the transfer of luminaire's heat are incorrect? **Check the two that apply.**
    a. Suspended fixtures transfer all their heat to the space, and they remain cool.
    b. Surfaced-mounted fixtures transfer all their heat to the space, and they remain cool.
    c. Surfaced-mounted fixtures transfer about 50% their heat to the space, and they run hot.
    d. Completely recessed and enclosed fixtures transfer about 50% of their heat to the plenum.
    e. Baffled or open louvered fixtures transfer about 75% of their heat to the plenum.

36. A tenant wants to install 2'x4' recessed light fixtures in an office. The floor area for the office is 1,200 s.f. Each fixture has four lamps. The tenant wants to have a lighting level of about 50 footcandles (fc) at desk level (3'-0" AFF). The luminaires can provide about 2,800 lumens per lamp at desk level. The coefficient of utilization (CU) is 60% when the fixtures are installed at 10'-0" above finish floor (AFF). Light loss factor (LLF) is 0.65. How many 2'x4' recessed light fixtures does the tenant need for this office?
    a. 12
    b. 14
    c. 16
    d. 18

37. For the same office and criteria in question 36, if the tenant uses 2-lamp 1'x4' fixtures instead of the 2'x4' recessed light fixtures, and these luminaires can provide about 3,000 lumens per lamp at desk level, how many 1'x4' light fixtures does the tenant need for this office?
    a. 26
    b. 28
    c. 30
    d. 32

38. For the same office and criteria in question 36, if utilities cost $5 per year for every 1,000 lumens, how much is the tenant utility cost for this office per month?
    a. $15
    b. $20
    c. $25
    d. $30

39. For the same office in question 36, if the cost of installation, labor, and materials is $300 for each 2'x4' recessed light fixture, how much is the tenant cost for installing all the lights in this office?
    a. $3,600
    b. $4,200
    c. $4,800
    d. $5,400

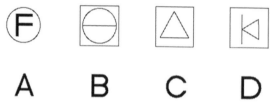

Figure 3.8 Electrical Symbols

40. Which symbol in figure 3.8 is a floor special purpose outlet?
    a. A
    b. B
    c. C
    d. D

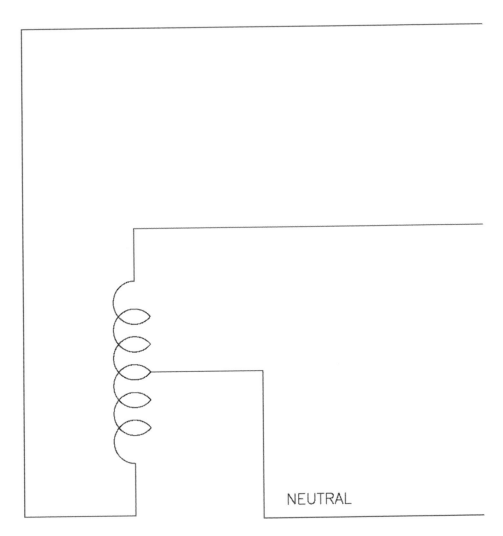

Figure 3.9   Wiring Diagram

41. What is the term for the wiring system in figure 3.9?
    a. single-phase, 3-wire service
    b. double-phase, 3-wire service
    c. three-phase, 3-wire service
    d. none of the above

Figure 3.10   Electrical Symbol

42. What is the term for the electrical symbol in figure 3.10?
    a. jack box
    b. junction box
    c. jack hammer
    d. j switch

43. An architect is working on a shopping center. One of the tenants requires 1200A, 277/480 V, 3-phase, 4-wire electrical service. The architect wants to verify if the electrical engineer has provided the requested service on the plans. Where can the architect find this information? **Check the three that apply.**
    a. electrical lighting plans
    b. single-line diagram
    c. panel schedules
    d. low-voltage plans
    e. power plans

44. In the design development phase of a design-bid-build project, an architect has received the mechanical roof plan and HVAC equipment schedules. Which of the project team members should the architect forward this information to for coordination? **Check the three that apply.**
    a. plumbing engineer
    b. electrical engineer
    c. structural engineer
    d. contractor
    e. civil engineer
    f. fire protection engineer

45. A credit card company has purchased a 15-year-old concrete tilt-up warehouse building. The company wants to remodel the warehouse as an office building. Additional HVAC equipment is necessary to provide comfort for building occupants. There is no as-built information for the building. What is the most cost-effective way to achieve this goal?
    a. Add additional columns and beams to support the additional weight of the new HVAC equipment.
    b. Do an X-ray of the building structure to find out if it can support the additional weight of the new HVAC equipment.
    c. Place the additional HVAC equipment on a concrete pad on grade outside of the building and install new ducts to the new HVAC equipment.
    d. Place the new HVAC equipment right on top of the existing structural columns.

46. A fan coil unit (FCU) is
    a. a simple device consisting of a heating or cooling coil and fan
    b. a fire-safety system
    c. an evaporative cooling system
    d. a hot-water recirculation system

47. Which of the following statements are true? **Check the two that apply.**
    a. A dry pipe fire sprinkler system is one in which the pipes are filled with pressurized air, rather than water.
    b. A dry pipe fire sprinkler system is one in which the pipes are filled with pressurized Halon, rather than water.
    c. A dry pipe fire sprinkler system is lighter and less expensive to install than a wet-pipe sprinkler system
    d. A dry pipe fire sprinkler system will not freeze in unheated spaces.
    e. A dry pipe fire sprinkler system has fewer valves and fittings to maintain.

48. Which of the following statements are true? **Check the two that apply.**
    a. The pressure relief valve (PRV) is a type of valve used to control or limit the pressure in a vessel or system.
    b. The PRV is designed or set to open at a predetermined set pressure to protect the system.
    c. The fluid (liquid, gas, or liquid–gas mixture) released from the PRV is usually routed through a piping system known as the *blowdown.*
    d. The pressure in a vessel or system typically needs to drop 30% below the predetermined set pressure before the valve resets.

49. An architect needs to calculate the U-value (overall thermal transmittance) for a wall assembly. Based on the following data, what is the U-value for the wall?

Component	R-value
Outside air layer	0.17
3/4" Cement plaster, sand aggregate	0.15
½" Plywood	0.62
Nominal 6" batt fiberglass	19.00
Gypsum board	0.45
Inside air layer	0.68

    a. approximately 0.02
    b. approximately 0.05
    c. approximately 0.08
    d. approximately 0.10

50. For the same wall in question 49, if the nominal 6" batt fiberglass is changed to nominal 3" batt fiberglass with an R-value of 11, and all other criteria stay the same, what is the U-value for the wall?
    a. approximately 0.02
    b. approximately 0.05
    c. approximately 0.08
    d. approximately 0.10

51. Entropy is
   a. the overall mass of a building assembly
   b. a thermodynamic property
   c. the total loss of heat when transferred through the building envelop
   d. the color of the roof

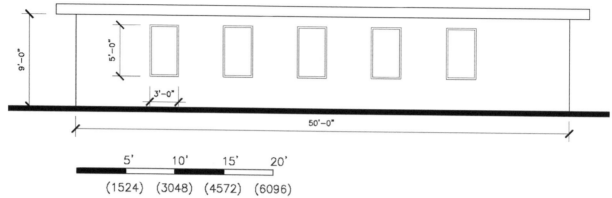

Figure 3.11   South Elevation of a Building

52. Figure 3.11 shows the south elevation of a building. If the U-value for the windows is 0.35, and the R-value for the opaque wall is 21, what is the overall U-value for the entire south wall of the building?
   a. approximately 0.05
   b. approximately 0.08
   c. approximately 0.10
   d. approximately 0.15

53. For the same south elevation shown in figure 3.11, if the U-value for the windows is 0.35, and overall U-value for the entire south wall is 0.086, what is the R-value for the opaque wall?
   a. approximately 13
   b. approximately 19
   c. approximately 30
   d. approximately 35

54. An architect is working on a theater project in California. There is a conflict between the *ADAAG Manual* and the California Building Code for handicap accessible ramp requirements. The local code has the same requirements as the California Building Code on this issue. What is a proper action for the architect?
   a. Comply with the California Building Code.
   b. Comply with the local code and California Building Code.
   c. Comply with the *ADAAG Manual*
   d. Comply with the most stringent or restrictive code

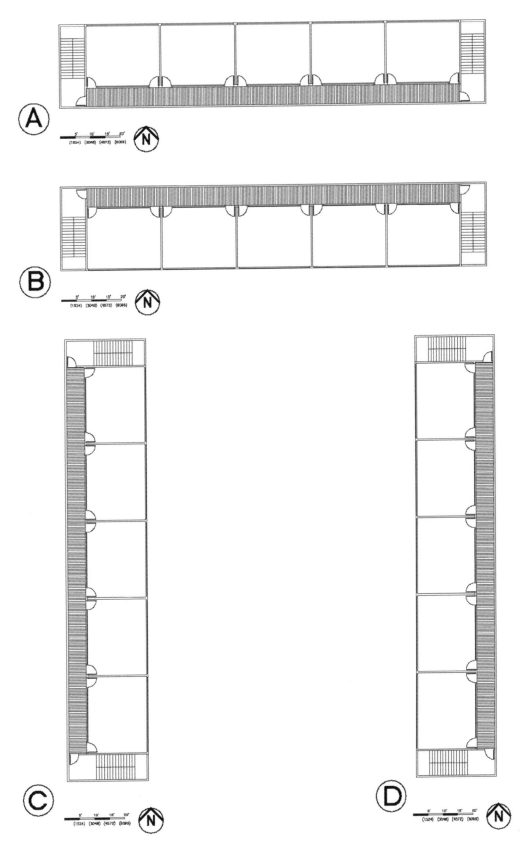

Figure 3.12   Orientation of a Classroom Building

55. An architect is working on a classroom building in the Northern Hemisphere. The teachers and students want the classroom to be energy efficient, and have the greatest potential to view outside with minimum window blind use. Which of the options in figure 3.12 is the best orientation for the classroom building to meet the demand of the teachers and students?
    a. A
    b. B
    c. C
    d. D

56. The R-value of a wall assembly includes resistance allowances for the following factors: **Check the two that apply.**
    a. time of day
    b. orientation
    c. insulation
    d. exterior air film

57. The principal effect of absorptive materials is on
    a. transmitted sound
    b. reflected sound
    c. transmitted sound and reflected sound
    d. none of the above

58. A simple test in construction is to blow smoke through a material. The purpose of this test is to
    a. determine if the material is watertight
    b. determine if the material is airtight
    c. determine if the material is a good sound absorbent
    d. none of the above

59. Which of the following statements are true? **Check the two that apply.**
    a. The thickness of felt absorbent has almost no impact on high-frequency sound.
    b. The thickness of felt absorbent has almost no impact on low-frequency sound.
    c. Once the sound frequency goes above 1 kHz, the variation of felt absorbent thickness has almost no impact on sound absorption.
    d. Once the sound frequency goes below 1 kHz, the variation of felt absorbent thickness has almost no impact on sound absorption.

60. An architect is designing a classroom. The optimum reverberation time is 0.35 seconds and, the classroom is 22'-0" wide, 20'-0" long, and 12'-0" high. What should the total room absorption be to achieve optimum reverberation time?
    a. approximately 250 sabins
    b. approximately 500 sabins
    c. approximately 750 sabins
    d. approximately 1000 sabins

61. A normal human being can hear sound in the range of
    a. 20 Hz to 2,000 Hz
    b. 20 Hz to 20,000 Hz
    c. 200 Hz to 20,000 Hz
    d. 200 Hz to 30,000 Hz

62. In a lecture hall, reflecting panels can (**Check the two that apply.**)
    a. help listeners hear the speaker with loudness and clarity
    b. reduce echoes
    c. increase sound absorption
    d. provide extra surfaces for image projection

63. A ray diagram is
    a. for analyzing the light effect
    b. for analyzing the heat transfer
    c. for analyzing the laser effect
    d. for analyzing reflected sound distribution

64. Which of the following sites is less noisy? **Check the two that apply.**
    a. a site behind a single row of high cypress trees
    b. a site behind several rows of high cypress trees
    c. a site in an open area
    d. a site between tall buildings

65. Which of the following statements are true? **Check the two that apply.**
    a. Nonthermal products cause most of the deaths in building fires.
    b. Thermal products cause most of the deaths in building fires.
    c. In the United States, most fires are now extinguished with one to three sprinklers operating.
    d. In the United States, most fires are now extinguished with one to five sprinklers operating.

66. BAS is
    a. the Baseline Analysis System
    b. the Building Automation System
    c. a unit to measure the loudness of sound
    d. a unit to measure heat generated by building fires

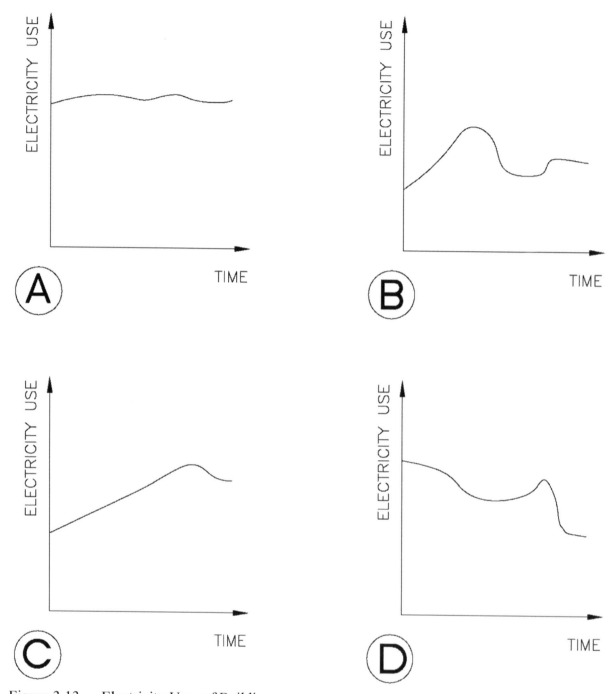

Figure 3.13   Electricity Uses of Buildings

67. Figure 3.13 shows the energy use of four "all-electrical" buildings with the same floor area and location at 32 degrees north of the Equator. Which building will benefit the most from seeking LEED certification?
    a. A
    b. B
    c. C
    d. D

68. Which of the following statements are not true? **Check the two that apply.**
    a. Double-deck elevators will save building space.
    b. All hydraulic elevators require a "hole" or an in-ground cylinder.
    c. Hydraulic elevators normally have a counter-weight.
    d. Traction-type elevators normally have a counter-weight.

69. Formaldehyde, small particles, carbon monoxide, radon, asbestos, and nicotine found in the indoor air of a building are classified as
    a. ventilation by-products
    b. building material emissions
    c. off-gas
    d. indoor air contaminants

70. Which of the following is an effective building lightning protection solution?
    I. a system of lightning rods and conductors connected to antennas
    II. a system of overhead conductors connected to the ground
    III. a system of lightning rods connected to the building's steel beams, columns, and ground

    a. I and II only
    b. I and III only
    c. II and III only
    d. I, II, and III

71. The persistence of sound in a particular space after the original sound has been removed is called:
    a. creep
    b. dampening
    c. frequency
    d. reverberation
    e. sound rebound
    f. echo

72. The drawings for the fire sprinkler system of a retail building are typically prepared by **(Check the two that apply)**:
    a. a mechanical engineer
    b. a plumbing engineer
    c. a fire protection consultant
    d. a fire protection sub-contractor

73. Which of the following are typically shown on low voltage drawings? **Check the two that apply.**
    a. fluorescent light fixtures
    b. incandescent light fixtures
    c. security cameras
    d. security alarms

74. In calculating light levels, the percentage of total lamp lumens that reach the work plane is defined as_____.

75. Which of the following are recoverable light loss factors? **Check the two that apply.**
    a. lamp lumen depreciation (LLD)
    b. lamp burnouts
    c. ambient fixture temperature
    d. supply voltage variation

76. An architect wants to find out the tonnage, weights, brand, and type of HVAC units being used in a building. Where can she most likely find all this information?
    a. the mechanical equipment schedule
    b. the mechanical roof plans
    c. the plumbing roof plans
    d. the architectural roof plans

77. A unit of sound absorption is called a_____.
    a. decibel
    b. bel
    c. sound wave
    d. sabin

78. ASHRAE stands for_____.
    a. The American Society of Heating, Refrigerating, and Air Conditioning Engineering
    b. The American Society of Heating, Refrigerating, and Air Conditioning Engineers
    c. The American Society of Heating, Refrigerating, and Air Control Engineering
    d. The American Society of Heating, Refrigerating, and Air Control Engineers

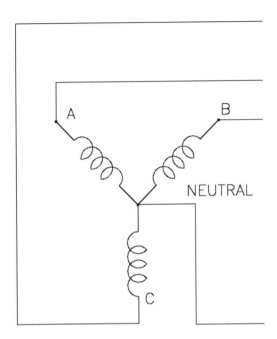

Figure 3.14   Electrical Wiring Diagram

79. The electrical wiring diagram in figure 3.14 can be for (**Check the two that apply.**)
    a. 120-V, single-phase, 2-wire service
    b. 120/240 V, single-phase, 3-wire service
    c. 120/208 V, 3-phase, 4-wire service
    d. 277/480 V, 3-phase, 4-wire service

80. Which of the following statements are true? **Check the two that apply.**
    a. A solid grounded neutral is never interrupted by switches or other devices.
    b. A solid grounded neutral can be interrupted by switches or other devices.
    c. A green ground wire is more effective than a ground-fault circuit interrupter.
    d. A ground-fault circuit interrupter is more effective than a green ground wire.

81. An architect found an electrical symbol on the electrical plans which read "20 amp, 250 V, 2 pole grounded outlet." What does pole mean?
    a. switch
    b. contact
    c. circuit
    d. hole

82. In electrical wiring design, it is often necessary to estimate the total building load. Which of the following will not affect the building load estimate?
    a. type of occupancy
    b. type of air conditioning
    c. future growth
    d. area of the space
    e. the actual number of users in the space

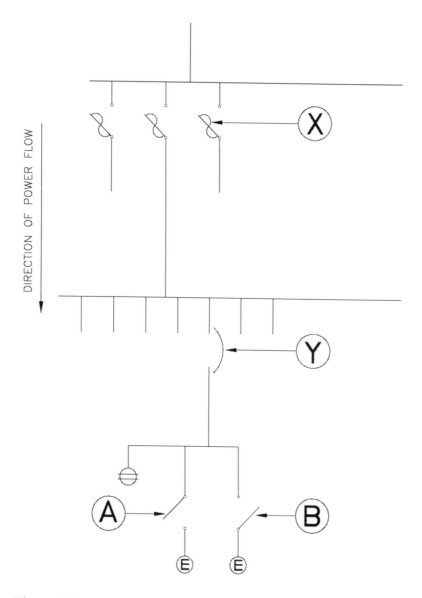

Figure 3.15   Electrical Wiring Diagram

83. What does X designate in figure 3.15?
    a. a switch
    b. a fused disconnect switch
    c. a circuit breaker
    d. a bus

84. What does Y designate in figure 3.15?
    a. a switch
    b. a fused disconnect switch
    c. a circuit breaker
    d. a bus

85. Which item is incorrectly connected in the electrical wiring diagram of figure 3.15?
    a. A
    b. B
    c. X
    d. Y

86. If light is considered a wave, the color of light is determined by its _____.

87. Which of the following shows an order from low frequency to high frequency?
    a. x-ray, infrared, visible light, ultraviolet, radar, radio
    b. x-ray, ultraviolet, visible light, infrared, radio, radar
    c. radio, radar, infrared, visible light, ultraviolet, x-ray
    d. radio, radar, ultraviolet, visible light, infrared, x-ray

88. Which of the following is not related to life-cycle costing for a given site?
    a. unscheduled maintenance
    b. renewal and replacement
    c. construction cost
    d. land cost
    e. energy costs
    f. minor repair

89. If we place a 1 candela (candlepower) source at the center of a transparent sphere with a one-meter radius, the amount of luminous energy emanating from one square meter of the surface of the sphere is _____.

90. Which of the following is not related to the human ability to see an object?
    a. size of the object
    b. familiarity with the object
    c. lighting
    d. disability glare
    e. the observer
    f. none of the above

91. One of the reasons that the ceiling and upper walls of rooms are often painted with light colors is
    a. to make the ceiling and walls maintenance free
    b. to make the ceiling and walls easy to clean
    c. to make the glare from ceiling lights less objectionable
    d. none of the above

92. Which of the following is not a component of total daylight factor?
    a. sky component
    b. externally reflected component
    c. reflected skylight
    d. reflected groundlight
    e. none of the above

93. Which of the following mandates minimum efficacy in lumens per watt and minimum color rendering index for fluorescent lamp types?
    a. The National Energy Policy Act of 1992 (EPAct)
    b. Illuminating Engineering Society of North America (IESNA)Standard 90.1-2007
    c. EPA
    d. USGBC

94. Fluorescent lamps with efficacies of about 85 lm/W are one of the most efficient light sources available. They convert about _____ percent of their energy to useful light.

95. Which of the following is not a type of high-intensity discharge (HID) lamps?
    a. fluorescent
    b. mercury
    c. metal-halide
    d. sodium-vapor

B. Mock Exam: BS Graphic Vignette Section

1. Directions and code

The **directions, codes,** and lighting diagrams are the same as the Mechanical &Electrical Plan sample vignette in the official NCARB ARE 4.0BS exam guide. The NCARB **directions** and **codes** have been very consistent throughout various versions of the ARE.

You can download the official exam guide and practice program for BDCS division at the following link:
http://www.ncarb.org/en/ARE/Preparing-for-the-ARE.aspx

2. Program

1) A reflected ceiling plan for a medical office is to be prepared. The space is in a multistory building and is enclosed by leasable office space on two sides, a corridor on another, and one exterior wall. The client wants a comfortable environment, efficient lighting levels, and flexibility for furniture placement (figure 3.16).

Note:
For your convenience, we have placed the DWG file for figure 3.16 on our website at: http://GreenExamEducation.com/

Here are the simple steps for you to download the DWG file for FREE:
- *Go to http://GreenExamEducation.com/*
- *Click on "Free Downloads and Forums" on the top menu*
- *Follow the instructions on the next page.*

2) Provide a 2'x4' grid with lay-in acoustical tiles in all spaces.
3) All ceiling heights are 9 ft above the finished floor.
4) For all spaces, use only recessed fluorescent fixtures to provide uniform light distribution with a light level of approximately 50 footcandles measured at desk level (3 ft above the finished floor).
5) Locate the accent light fixtures along the south wall of the Waiting Area so that the direct light level in the wall at a height of 5 ft above the floor is 80 footcandles.
6) Rigid ducts do **not** fit through joists or between the bottom of joists and the ceiling. Rigid ducts fit under beams and in spaces between joists.
7) Rigid ducts that run **perpendicular** to joists must be within 2'-0" of a beam or bearing wall.
8) Connect each supply diffuser to the rigid supply duct system with flexible duct, even when the diffuser is right under the rigid supply duct.
9) Flexible duct lengths shall not exceed 10 ft.
10) Flexible ducts fit through joist webs.
11) Provide as much separation between the supply air diffusers and return air grille as possible.
12) Provide one supply diffuser and one return-air grille for every 144 s.f. of floor area (or portion thereof) in each space.

3. Time

You must complete the vignette within 1 hour.

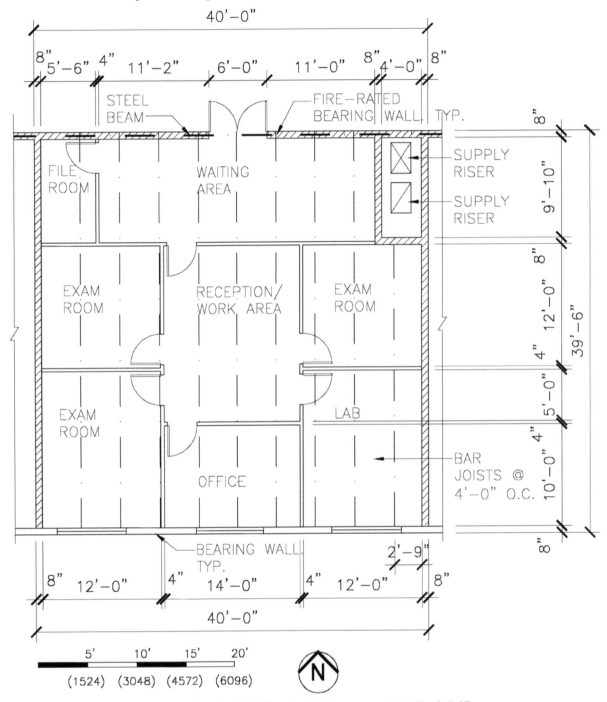

Figure 3.16   Plan for the Mechanical &Electrical Vignette: a Medical Office

Chapter Four

ARE Mock Exam Solutions for the
Building Systems (BS) Division

A. Mock Exam Answers and Explanations: BS Multiple-Choice (MC) Section

Note: If you answer 60% of the questions correctly, you will pass the MC Section of the exam.

1. Answer: <u>5,000</u> dollars.
    The following is a step-by-step solution:

    a) The owner's design criteria require 10,000 BTU per 300 s.f. of gross area (2,930.71 W per 27.87 s.m.).

        An office with 1,500 s.f. (139.35 s.m.) of gross area needs:
        (1,500 s.f./300 s.f.) x 10,000 BTU = 50,000 BTU (14,653.55 W)

    b) In the question, "**ton**" refers to one "**ton of cooling**," a common HVAC unit in North America. This is 12,000 BTU/h or the amount of power needed to melt one **short ton** (2,000 pounds or 907 kilograms or 907 kg) of ice in 24 hours (approximately 3.52 kw).

        *Note: Please pay attention to the difference between a **short ton**, a **long ton** and a **metric ton**. A **short ton** is 2,000 pounds or 907 kg; a **long ton** is 2,240 pounds or 1,016 kg; and a **metric ton** is 2,205 lb or 1,000 kg.*

        *If a **metric ton** or a **long ton** is used, it is specifically noted.*

        50,000 BTU/12,000 BTU = 4.16 ton

    c) Since the HVAC system is only available in an integer ton, the smallest HVAC unit we can choose is a 5-ton unit.

        The stated market price of a central air-conditioning system is $1,000 per ton, so the minimum cost of a HVAC system for the office that meets the owner's criteria is:

        $1,000 x 5 = $5,000 or <u>5,000</u> dollars.

        Note: This is NOT an easy calculation problem and you may have come up with the right answer for the wrong reasons. We place it at the beginning of the mock exam to test your time management skills. If you spend too much time on this question, you will NOT have enough time to finish the rest of the questions. I suggest you mark ANY calculation problem that requires more than 30 seconds of your time, pick a guess answer, and then move on to other questions. Go back and complete the marked calculation problems AFTER you finish other questions if you have extra time.

This is an important tip for you to pass ANY ARE exam.

2. Answer: 1/4" x 90 = 22.5" =1'-10 ½" or 1.875 feet (571.50)

3. Answer: a
    Convection, thermal **radiation,** and heat **conduction** are three basic forms of heat transfer.

    The transfer of heat via the movement of **fluids** is called **convection**. **Convection** is the dominant form of heat transfer in liquids and gases.

    Thermal **radiation** is energy emitted by matter as electromagnetic waves. It is a direct result of the random movements of atoms and molecules in matter. It propagates without the presence of matter through the vacuum of space.

    Heat **conduction** is heat transfer via the interaction of hot atoms and molecules with neighboring atoms and molecules, transferring some of their energy (heat) to these neighboring particles or as electrons move from one atom to another. It is the main form of heat transfer within a solid or between solid objects.

    Mass transfer is the energy or heat transfer by physically moving a hot or cold object from one place to another, like placing hot water in a bottle or the movement of an iceberg in changing ocean currents.

4. Answer: b and c
    In plumbing, the unobstructed space between a wall mounted faucet and the sink rim is an air gap or the cheapest form of backflow prevention. This prevents siphonage.

    The handicap clearance answer is just a **distracter**.

5. Answer: d
    A diagram that illustrates the relationships between dry bulb temperature, wet bulb temperature, and relative humidity as well as other properties is called a **psychrometric chart**. A simple **psychrometric chart** can include **dry** bulb temperature lines (vertical lines), **wet** bulb temperature lines (diagonal lines), **dew point** temperature lines (horizontal lines), **relative humidity** lines (upward curved lines), and other properties.

    Choice "c", a human comfort factors chart, is a **distracter**. The environmental factors that affect human comfort include dry bulb temperature, humidity, mean radiant temperature, and air speed. Other factors include clothing and metabolism.

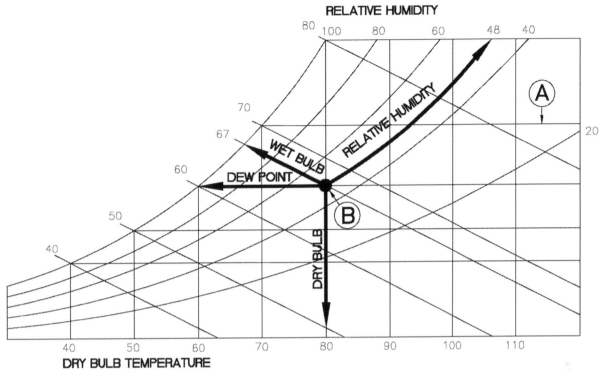

Figure 4.1   A Simple Psychrometric Chart (The temperatures are shown in °F, and the relative humidity is shown in percentages.)

6. Answer: The line labeled as "A" represents <u>a dew point temperature</u>.

Figure 4.1 and 3.1are simple **psychrometric charts.** Know how to read and use them. Understanding and memorizing what the lines represent is also a good idea.

As long as you know at least two of the properties in the chart, you can determine the others. For example, if you know the **dry** bulb temperature is 80°F and the **wet** bulb temperature is 67°F for a room, you can:
a) Locate the intersection (point "B") of the 80°F **dry** bulb temperature line and the 67°F **wet** bulb temperature line.
b) Follow the curved line from the intersection at point "B" to determine that the **relative humidity** is about 48%. You can use a dehumidifier to reduce the **relative humidity in a room** to 25% to 35% for better human comfort.
c) Determine that the **dew point temperature** is about 60°F by following the horizontal line from point "B". You need to keep the wall **temperature** above 60°F to prevent condensation (figure 4.1).

The example above is to show you the basic methods of how to read and use the chart. There are more detailed and computerized **psychrometric charts** available to assist people to obtaining data that are more accurate. However, the basic principles are the same for all **psychrometric charts**.

7. Answer: c
Per *ADAAG Manual: A Guide to the American with Disabilities Accessibility Guidelines*, the operable parts which are essential to the basic operation of a telephone can be a maximum of 54 inches above the floor for a side reach approach.

See the following link:
http://www.access-board.gov/adaag/html/figures/fig44.html

8. Answer: a and d
Please note that the question asks for statements that are NOT true.

The following statements regarding the electrical single line diagram are NOT true and therefore the correct answers:
- Elements on the diagram represent the physical size or location of the electrical equipment.
- Common convention does <u>not</u> dictate organization of the diagram with the same left-to-right, top-to-bottom sequence as the switchgear or other apparatus represented.

The following statements regarding electrical single line diagram are true:
- Elements on the diagram do <u>not</u> represent the physical size or location of the electrical equipment.
- Common convention dictates organization of the diagram with the same left-to-right, top-to-bottom sequence as the switchgear or other apparatus represented.

9. Answer: b, c, d, and e
The human body can lose heat through:
- **evaporation,** the transmission of heat via the process of moisture changing to vapor.
- **conduction,** the transmission of heat through direct contact.
- **convection**, the transmission of heat via the movement of a fluid (liquid or gas).
- **radiation,** the transmission of heat through electromagnetic waves from a warm surface to a cooler surface.

Ventilation and condensation are just distracters.

10. Answer: b
Figure 3.2 shows a variable flow system.
- **A single zone system** delivers conditioned air to various spaces at a constant temperature and low velocity.
- **A variable flow system** uses a damper and thermostat at outlets to control airflow.
- **A double duct system** uses separate ducts to deliver warm and cool air to a terminal mixing box with a damper controlled by a thermostat.
- **A terminal reheat system** provides air at about 55°F (12°C) to terminals with hot water reheat coils.

11. Answer: a and d
    Please note that the question asks for statements that are NOT true.

    The main purpose of the question is to test your knowledge on the difference between heat pumps and packaged air-conditioning units.

    Heat pumps (NOT Packaged air-conditioning units) are electrically powered heating and cooling units. Cooling for heat pumps is NOT provided by outdoor condensing units. For packaged air-conditioning units (NOT heat pumps), cooling is provided by outdoor condensing units, heating is provided by an oil or gas furnace, OR electric resistance heaters. So, it is a mistake to generalize and state: "Packaged air-conditioning units) are electrically powered heating and cooling units."

    Packaged air-conditioning units and heat pumps are VERY common units and you should know them well. This will help you pass ARE exams and in real architectural practice.

12. Answer: **Water hammer** is a pressure surge that can occur when water is shut off or forced to change direction abruptly. It can cause noise, vibration, or pipe collapse. **Capped air chambers** or **manufactured shock absorbers** are often used at fixture branches to alleviate this problem.

13. Answer: c
    Capped air chamber is the term for X in figure 3.3. See the explanation to question 12 for further information. X is not an exhaust vent, a manufactured shock absorber, or a vent pipe.

14. Answer: a
    In a cold climate, the proper arrangement of building elements for an exterior wall from outside to inside is plaster, plywood, batt insulation, vapor barrier, water pipe, drywall.

    The key to answering this question correctly is that both the vapor barrier and water pipe have to be placed on the warm side of the room in winter. This is to prevent condensation and the water pipe from freezing in winter.

15. Answer: b and d
    The following statements are true:
    • Roof drains should be connected to a storm drain if possible.
    • A grease interceptor can be connected to a sewer line.

    Overflow drains should NEVER be connected to a storm drain. They should be spilled at about 8" above exterior grade and at locations that can be easily noticed by building users. Their purpose is to drain the rainwater from the roof if the roof drains become clogged. If rainwater starts to drain from the overflow drains, it means either the roof drains are clogged, or there is too much rain. Excessive ponding of rainwater could cause the roof to collapse; the building users should be able to notice this condition and have the problem fixed right away.

A floor drain can NEVER be connected to a sewer line. A floor drain collects graywater, while a sewer is for black water. These two distinct types of water should never be mixed together.

A grease interceptor can be connected to a sewer line because its purpose is to intercept the grease from kitchen sinks.

The following concepts are VERY important:

Potable water is clean water used for human consumption.

Graywater is household water that has not come into contact with kitchen sinks, human excretion, or animal waste. Graywater includes used water from bathroom washbasins, bathtubs, showers, and water from laundry tubs and clothes washers. Graywater does not include water from dishwashers or kitchen sinks.

Blackwater, otherwise known as brown water, foul water, or sewage, is water from the kitchen sink, dishwasher, or water that has come into contact with human or animal waste.

NEVER mix the plumbing system for potable water, graywater, or blackwater.

16. Answer: a and c
Rainwater and water from laundry tubs and clothes washers is **graywater**.

Water from dishwashers, kitchen sinks, and toilets is **blackwater**. See explanation to answer 15 for further information.

17. Answer: A pipe with a maximum of _5 ½_ inches outside diameter can fit inside a 6" wood stud wall.

A 6" <u>wood</u> stud wall is a <u>nominal</u> dimension, and the actual dimension of the wood stud is 5 ½". On the other hand, a 6" <u>metal</u> stud wall is a <u>real</u> dimension, and the actual dimension of the metal stud is 6".

18. Answer: c
A 2" copper pipe means the inner diameter of the pipe is a little larger than 2"due to historical reasons.

In the 1930s, the copper pipe was designated by its inner diameter and a 1⁄16" (1.6) wall thickness. For example, a 2-inch (50.80) copper pipe had a 2 1/8" (54.61) outside diameter. With the development of technology, pipe walls became thinner, but the outside diameter stayed the same so it could mate with existing older pipes, increasing the inner diameter beyond two inches.

The sizes and history of cast iron pipes and plastic pipes are similar.

19. Answer: Receptacles in wet locations should be protected by a <u>ground fault interrupter (GFI)</u>. A GFI device breaks the circuit immediately when current leakage occurs. It can be a GFI breaker at the service panel or a GFI receptacle.

20. Answer: d

The electrical symbol in figure 3.4 represents a generator. See *Architectural Graphic Standards (AGS)*. Make sure to look through the AGS sections that are related to the ARE BS division, and know what certain symbols represent.

21. Answer: d

Normally the minimum height of a vent pipe extension is 6" above the roof.
However, for a roof space accessible by the public or building tenants, the minimum height of a vent pipe extension is 7'-0" above the roof. See section 904.1 of the *International Plumbing Code*.

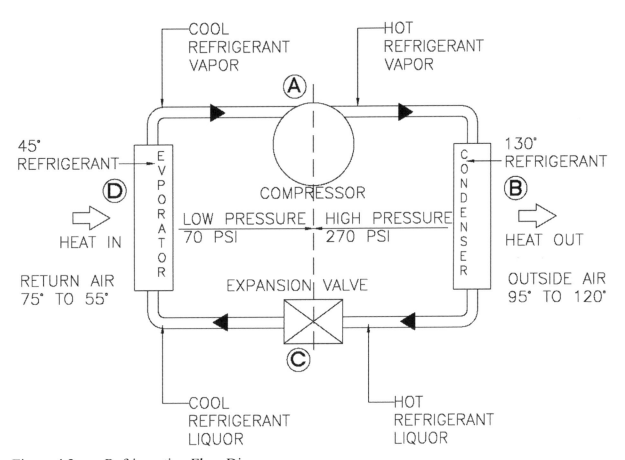

Figure 4.2   Refrigeration Flow Diagram

22. Answer: c
    In the refrigeration flow diagram (figure 3.5 and 4.2), the expansion valve is located at C.

    See the link below for a 1940's U.S. government film on the refrigeration cycle:
    http://www.youtube.com/watch?v=b527al9D_rY

    This video is old but very clearly explains the refrigeration cycle, and the heat transfer processes of conduction, convection, and radiation.

    Similar information and diagrams can be found in *Architectural Graphic Standards (AGS)*.

23. Answer: b
    For a faucet in a house, a globe valve is most likely used.

    The following are some common valve types and their uses:

    - A **gate valve** is used where control is either completely off or on, and has a low friction loss.
    - A **globe valve** is used where water is frequently controlled and water flow varies such as at hose bibs or faucets, and has a high friction loss.
    - A **check valve** allows water to flow in only one direction, preventing back flow and related water contamination.
    - An **angle valve** is a globe valve with a built-in 90-degree turn.
    - A **butterfly valve** is used for on-off operation of gas, water, air, and vacuum line. This valve features a quarter-turn. In homes, it is often used as the shut-off valve near the water or gas meter.

    See AGS for images of the different types of valves and be able to identify them by their image.

24. Answer: a and c
    Occupants (body heat) and air infiltration (convection of hot outside air) may be a source of a building's heat gain.

    Lightning (NOT lighting) and insulation is NOT a source of a building's heat gain.

25. Answer: a
    A 120/240 V, single-phase, three-wire system is common for residences or smaller buildings; 240 V is for dryers and electric ranges.

    A120/208 V, three-phase, four-wire system is frequently used for larger buildings and provides a variety of electrical loads.

    A 277/480 V, three-phase, four-wire system is for even larger buildings, especially buildings with 277 V <u>fluorescent</u> lights, such as offices or shops. This system requires smaller, step-down transformers to provide 120 V services for outlets.

A 2400/4160 V, three-phase, four-wire system is for factories with machinery or very large commercial buildings.

26. Answer: b and d
Urinals and toilets contain human waste and are permitted to connect to a **soil stack vent**.

Lavatories and bidets do <u>NOT</u> contain human waste and are permitted to connect to a **waste stack vent**.

27. Answer: c
Underground water lines should be placed below the frost line to avoid freezing.

28. Answer: c
A handicapped accessible receptacle outlet is a minimum of 15" above the floor

Per *ADAAG Manual: A Guide to the American with Disabilities Accessibility Guidelines*, section 4.27.3, electrical and communications system receptacles on walls shall be mounted no less than 15 in (380 mm) above the floor.

29. Answer: d
Glass has the lowest coefficient of thermal expansion.

The coefficients of thermal expansion for some common piping material are as follows:
- PVC: 52
- Copper: 17
- Iron: 11.8
- Glass: 8.5

See the following link for further information:
http://en.wikipedia.org/wiki/Thermal_expansion

30. Answer: b
The solar altitude is <u>largest</u> in the <u>Northern</u> Hemisphere on the day of the <u>summer</u> solstice and smallest on the day of winter solstice. <u>Summer</u> solstice is the day of the year with the longest period of daylight, while winter solstice is the day of the year with the shortest period of daylight.

These days are exactly the opposite in the Southern Hemisphere.

On the equinox (vernal and autumnal), night and day are roughly the same lengths.

31. Answer: b and c
Figure 3.6 indicates the use of two single-pole, double-throw switches and one four-way switch to control lighting from three locations.

32. Answer: b
The term for Z in figure 3.7 is acoustical lining. It reduces noise buildup inside the machine.

33. Answer: c and e
Pay attention to the word "not."

Putting acoustical lining outside of the HVAC ducts or using stainless steel ducts are not effective ways to control noise between two adjacent apartment units, and are therefore the correct answers.

However, flexible boots, resilient hangers and acoustical lining inside of the HVAC ducts are effective ways to control noise between two adjacent apartment units, and are therefore the incorrect answers.

34. Answer: a and c
The following statements are true:
• Duct silencers and baffles are normally placed inside the HVAC ducts.
• Duct silencers and baffles are useful to reduce fan noise but cause considerable pressure drop.

35. Answer: b and c
We are looking for incorrect statements.
The following statements regarding fixture installation and the transfer of luminaire's heat are false and therefore the correct answers:
• Surfaced-mounted fixtures transfer all their heat to the space, and they remain cool.
• Surfaced-mounted fixtures transfer about 50% their heat to the space, and they run hot. (They transfer all their heat to the space, but run hot because this transfer is blocked upward.)

The following statements regarding fixture installation and the transfer of luminaire's heat are true and therefore the incorrect answers:
• Suspended fixtures transfer all their heat to the space, and they remain cool.
• Completely recessed and enclosed fixtures transfer about 50% of their heat to the plenum.
• Baffled or open louvered fixtures transfer about 75% of their heat to the plenum.

36. Answer: b

The tenant needs fourteen (14) recessed light fixtures for this office.

Based on the NCARB Building Systems division list of references and formulas sheet (BSreferences.pdf, available in the real exam) and our discussions on page 24, we can do the following calculations:

Lumens per fixture= (lumens per lamp) x (number of lamps per fixture) =
2,800 x 4 =11,200

Number of 2'x4' recessed light fixtures = Number of luminaires = (footcandles) x (floor area) / (lumens per fixture) x (CU) x (LLF) = 50 x 1,200 /11,200 x 0.60 x 0.65 =13.73 or about 14.

37. Answer: a

The tenant needs twenty-six (26) 1'x4' light fixtures for this office.

Lumens per fixture= (lumens per lamp) x (number of lamps per fixture) =
3,000 x 2 = 6,000

Number of 1'x4' light fixtures = Number of luminaires = (footcandles) x (floor area) / (lumens per fixture) x (CU) x (LLF) = 50 x 1,200 /6,000 x 0.60 x 0.65 = 25.64 or about 26.

38. Answer: c

The tenant utility cost for this office is $25 per month.

Footcandles [lux] = lumens / area in s.f. (s.m.)

Lumens = footcandles [lux] x [area in s.f. (s.m.)] = 50 x 1,200 = 60,000

Utilities cost per year = (60,000/1,000) x 5 = $300
Utilities cost per month = Utilities cost per year/12 = 300/12 = $25

39. Answer: b

Since the tenant needs fourteen (14) recessed light fixtures for this office, the tenant cost for installing all the lights in this office = 14 x $300 = $4,200.

40. Answer: c

Symbol C in figure 3.8 is a floor special purpose outlet.

The correct terms for the other symbols are as follows:
- A: fan hanger receptacle
- B: floor single receptacle outlet
- C: floor special purpose outlet
- D: floor telephone outlet-private

Look through the *Architectural Graphic Standards (AGS)* and become familiar with the symbols used in electrical, mechanical, and plumbing plans.

41. Answer: a

The term for the wiring system in figure 3.9 is single-phase, 3-wire service.

Look through *Mechanical and Electrical Equipment for Buildings* (MEEB), and study all the **images, diagrams, and charts**. Read the related text if you find a diagram or chart confusing.

42. Answer: b
Junction box is the term for J in figure 3.10.

43. Answer: b, c, and e
The architect can find electrical service information on the:
- single-line diagram
- panel schedules
- power plans

Electrical lighting plans and low voltage plans do not contain electrical service information on them.

As an architect, you need to know enough about your consultants' work to be able to coordinate with them.

44. Answer: a, b, and c
The architect should forward the mechanical roof plan and HVAC equipment schedules received during design development to the following project team members for coordination:
- The plumbing engineer provides condensation lines for the rooftop HVAC units.
- The electrical engineer supplies power for the rooftop HVAC units.
- The structural engineer makes sure the structure can support the rooftop HVAC units.

The architect should NOT forward the information to the following project team members:
- The contractor does not get involved until the project is out to bid for a design-bid-build project.
- The civil engineer does not need rooftop HVAC unit information.
- The fire protection engineer does not need to coordinate the rooftop HVAC units for typical buildings.

45. Answer: c
The most cost-effective way to achieve this goal is to place the additional HVAC equipment on a concrete pad at grade outside of the building and install new ducts to this equipment.

Adding additional columns and beams to support the additional weight of the new HVAC equipment is NOT cost-effective.

Having an X-ray taken of the building structure to find out if it can support the additional weight of the new HVAC equipment is very expensive.

Placing the new HVAC equipment right on top of the existing structural columns may not provide adequate structural support, and the columns may conflict with the HVAC supply or return ducts.

46. Answer: a

A **fan coil unit (FCU)** is a simple device consisting of a heating or cooling coil and fan. A FCU is part of an HVAC system, and typically NOT connected to ductwork. Either a thermostat or a manual on/off switch controls the device.

47. Answer: a and d

The following statements are true:
- A dry pipe fire sprinkler system is one in which the pipes are filled with pressurized air, rather than water.
- A dry pipe fire sprinkler system will not freeze in unheated spaces.

The following statements are false:
- A dry pipe fire sprinkler system is one in which the pipes are filled with pressurized Halon, rather than water.
- A dry pipe fire sprinkler system is lighter and less expensive to install than a wet-pipe sprinkler system
- A dry pipe fire sprinkler system has fewer valves and fittings to maintain.

48. Answer: a and b

The following statements are true:
- The pressure relief valve (PRV) is a type of valve used to control or limit the pressure in a vessel or system.
- The PRV is designed to open at a predetermined set pressure to protect the system.

The following statements are false:
- The fluid (liquid, gas, or liquid–gas mixture) released from the PRV is usually routed through a piping system known as the *blowdown*. (The *blowdown* is a percentage of set pressure and refers to how much the pressure needs to drop before the valve reseats.)
- The pressure in a vessel or system typically needs to drop 30% below the predetermined set pressure before the valve resets. (The pressure in a vessel or system typically needs to drop 2% to 20% below the predetermined set pressure before the valve reseats.)

49. Answer: b

The U-value for the wall is 0.0475 or approximately 0.05.

1) First seek the total resistance of the wall assembly (R_t) by adding together the R-values for each wall component.

Component	R-value
Outside air layer	0.17
3/4" Cement plaster, sand aggregate	0.15
½" Plywood	0.62
Nominal 6" batt fiberglass	19.00
Gypsum board	0.45
Inside air layer	0.68
R_t	**21.07**

2) The U-value of the wall assembly is then calculated with the following equation:
   $U = 1/ R_t = 1/21.07 = 0.0475$

50. Answer: c
    The U-value for the wall is 0.0765 or approximately 0.08.

    1) First seek the total resistance of the wall assembly (R_t) by adding together the R-values for each wall component.

Component	R-value
Outside air layer	0.17
3/4" Cement plaster, sand aggregate	0.15
½" Plywood	0.62
Nominal 3" batt fiberglass	11.00
Gypsum board	0.45
Inside air layer	0.68
R_t	13.07

2) The U-value of the wall assembly is then calculated with the following equation:
   $U = 1/ R_t = 1/13.07 = 0.0765$

51. Answer: b
    Entropy is used to determine the energy available for useful work in a thermodynamic process, such as in engines, energy conversion devices, or machines.

52. Answer: c
    The overall U-value for the south wall of the building is approximately 0.10.

    $U_w = 0.35$

    $R_{op} = 21$
    $U_{op} = 1/21 = 0.048$

    $A_w = (3'-0" \times 5'-0") \times 5$ windows $= 75$ s.f.
    $A_o = 9'-0" \times 50'-0" = 450$ s.f.
    $A_{op} = A_o - A_w = 450$ s.f. $- 75$ s.f. $= 375$ s.f.

    Per the reference sheet provided by NCARB:
    $U_o = [(U_w \times A_w) + (U_{op} \times A_{op})]/A_o = [(0.35 \times 75) + (0.048 \times 375)]/450 = 0.098$ or approximately 0.10

53. Answer: c
    The R-value for the opaque wall is approximately 30.

    $U_w = 0.35$
    $U_o = 0.086$

A_w = (3'-0" x5'-0") x 5 windows= 75 s.f.
A_o= 9'-0" x 50'-0"= 450 s.f.
A_{op} = A_o– A_w = 450s.f.- 75 s.f. = 375 s.f.

Per the reference sheet provided by NCARB:
U_o= [(U_w x A_w) + (U_{op} x A_{op})]/A_o

U_o x A_o= (U_w x A_w) + (U_{op} x A_{op})

U_{op} x A_{op}= (U_o x A_o)– (U_w x A_w)

U_{op}=[(U_o x A_o) – (U_w x A_w)]/ A_{op} = [(0.086 x 450)–(0.35 x 75)]/375
= (38.7- 26.25)/375 =12.45/375 = 0.0332

R_{op}= 1/ U_{op} = 1/0.0332 = 30.10 or approximately 30

54. Answer: d
The architect should comply with the most stringent or restrictive code when there is a conflict between the federal, state (provincial), or local code.

55. Answer: a
Layout A shows the best orientation of the classroom building to meet the demand of the teachers and students:
- The long side of the building aligns with the east-west axis, and most of the windows face south or north.
- The corridor is placed on the south side. This will not only help block the high angle summer sun, but also allow the low angle winter sun into the classroom. The orientation also yields the greatest potential for outside views with minimum window blind use.
- The windows on the north side can fully utilize natural light with little or no direct sunlight.

56. Answer: c and d
The R-value of a wall assembly includes resistance allowances for insulation and the exterior air film.

The R-value of a wall assembly does NOT include resistance allowances for time of day or orientation.

57. Answer: b
The principal effect of absorptive materials is on reflected sound. Absorptive materials have little effect on transmitted sound.

58. Answer: c
A simple test in construction is to blow smoke through a material. The purpose of this test is to determine if the material is a good sound absorbent. If the material is porous, thick, fibrous, and allows smoke to pass freely, it should be a good sound absorbent.

59. Answer: a and c
The following statements are true:
- The thickness of felt absorbent has almost no impact on high-frequency sound.
- Once the sound frequency goes above 1 kHz, the variation of the thickness of felt absorbent has almost no impact on sound absorption.

60. Answer: c
The total room absorption should be approximately 75 sabins to achieve optimum reverberation time.

$T_R = 0.35$ s

$V = 22'\text{-}0'' \times 20'\text{-}0'' \times 12'\text{-}0'' = 5280$ ft^3

For English system: $K = 0.05$ (See the BS division PDF reference sheet downloaded from NCARB website listed on page 23.)

Based on NCARB reference sheet:
$T_R = K \times V/\sum A$

$\sum A = K \times V/T_R = 0.05 \times 5280/0.35 = 754.3$ or approximately 750 sabins.

61. Answer: b
A normal human being can hear sound in the range of 20 Hz to 20,000 Hz.

62. Answer: a and b
In a lecture hall, reflecting panels can help listeners to hear the speaker with loudness and clarity as well as reduce echoes.

Reflecting panels are unlikely to increase sound absorption or provide extra surfaces for image projection.

63. Answer: d
A **ray diagram** is for analyzing reflected sound distribution in a hall, using only the first reflection.

64. Answer: b and c
A site behind multiple rows of high cypress trees is more effective than a site protected by only a single row.

A site in an open area is much quieter than a site between tall buildings.

65. Answer: a and d
The following statements are true:

- Nonthermal products (smoke and gas) cause most of the deaths (about 75%) in building fires.
- In the United States, most fires are now extinguished with one to five sprinklers operating.

About 25% of deaths in building fires are caused by thermal products (flame and heat).

66. Answer: b
BAS stands for Building Automation System. The other choices are simply distracters.

67. Answer: A
Building A shown in figure 3.13 will most likely benefit the most from seeking LEED certification because it currently consumes the greatest amount of electricity of the four. Seeking LEED certification will likely reduce the energy use or electricity use for this building.

68. Answer: b and c
Please note the question asks for statements that are NOT true.

The following statements are false:
- All hydraulic elevators require a "hole" or an in-ground cylinder. (There are "hole-less" type hydraulic elevators.)
- Hydraulic elevators normally have a counter-weight.

The following statements are true:
- Double-deck elevators will save building space.
- Traction-type elevators normally have a counter-weight.

69. Answer: d
When found in a building's indoor air, formaldehyde, small particles, carbon monoxide, radon, asbestos, and nicotine are all classified as indoor-air contaminants.

Nicotine is from smoking. It is not a ventilation by-product, building-material emission, or off-gas.

70. Answer: c
II and III only

The following are effective solutions for building lightning protection:
- A system of overhead conductors connected to the ground.
- A system of lightning rods connected to the building's steel beams, columns, and ground.

A system of lightning rods and conductors connected to antennas is NOT an effective lightning protection solution because it is NOT connected to the ground.

71. Answer: d
The <u>persistence</u> of sound in a particular space after the original sound has been removed is called **reverberation**.

Creep is the tendency of a solid material to slowly move or deform permanently under the influence of stresses.

Dampening means to "make less strong or intense."

Frequency is the number of occurrences of a repeating event per unit time.

Echo is the reflection of a sound.

Sound rebound is a **distracter**.

72. Answer: c and d
The drawings for the fire sprinkler system of a retail building are typically prepared in one of two ways:
- The owner's fire protection consultant prepares a set of criteria drawings per the owner's requirements, and then a fire protection sub-contractor prepares the construction drawings based on them.

OR
- A fire protection sub-contractor can prepare the entire construction drawing set as part of his design-build contract without the involvement of the owner's fire protection consultant.

Neither a mechanical engineer nor a plumbing engineer prepares the fire sprinkler system of a building.

73. Answer: c and d
Security cameras and alarms are shown on low voltage drawings.

Fluorescent and incandescent light fixtures are typically shown on electrical lighting plans.

74. Answer: In calculating light levels, the percentage of total lamp lumens that reach the work plane is defined as <u>**the coefficient of utilization**</u>.

75. Answer: a and b
The following are recoverable light loss factors because they can be reduced by preventative maintenance:
- lamp lumen depreciation (LLD)
- lamp burnouts
- fixture (luminaire) dirt depreciation (LLD)
- room surface dirt depreciation (RSDD).

The following are non-recoverable light loss factors because they cannot be reduced by preventative maintenance:

- ambient fixture temperature
- supply voltage variation
- ballast factor
- optical factor
- fixture surface depreciation.

76. Answer: a

If an architect wants to find out the tonnage, weights, brand, and type of HVAC units being used in a building, she can find all this information on the mechanical equipment schedule.

Mechanical roof plans only have some of the HVAC unit information such as the tonnage and weights.

Neither plumbing roof plans nor architectural roof plans have specific HVAC unit information.

77. Answer: d

A unit of sound absorption is called a **sabin**. One square meter of 100% absorbing material equals one metric sabin.

78. Answer: b

ASHRAE stands for <u>The American Society of Heating, Refrigerating, and Air Conditioning Engineers</u>.

79. Answer: c and d

Figure 3.14 can be the electrical wiring diagram for 120/208 V, 3-phase, 4-wire service or 277/480 V, 3-phase, 4-wire service.

80. Answer: a and d

The following statements are true:

- Switches or other devices never interrupt a solid grounded neutral.
- A ground-fault circuit interrupter is more effective than a green ground wire.

To prevent shocks, a ground-fault circuit interrupter will completely cut off the current in about a half- second if there is a short circuit. A green ground wire will still allow a small amount of "shock" current to pass through in the event of a failure. A green ground wire can allow the ground fault to "leak" and can cause fire or equipment damages.

81. Answer: c

An architect found an electrical symbol on the electrical plans which read "20 amp, 250 V, 2 pole grounded outlet." Pole means circuit in this situation.

The terms "pole" and "throw" are common in switch contact variations. The number of "poles" is the number of separate circuits controlled by a switch. The number of "throws" is the number of separate positions the switch can adopt.

82. Answer: e
   Pay attention to the word "not."

   In electrical wiring design, it is often necessary to estimate the total building load. The <u>actual</u> number of users in the space will <u>not</u> affect the building load estimate, and is therefore the correct answer.

   The number of <u>estimated</u> occupants based on the type of occupancy and area of the space will affect the building load estimate.

   The following will affect the building load estimate, and are therefore the incorrect answers:
   • type of occupancy
   • type of air conditioning
   • future growth
   • area of the space

83. Answer: b
   X in figure 3.15 is a fused disconnect switch.

84. Answer: c
   Y in figure 3.15 is a circuit breaker.

85. Answer: a
   Item A is incorrectly connected in figure 3.15.

   Switches should be connected with the "dead" blade, NOT the "hot" blade with electrical current.

86. Answer: If light is considered a wave, the color of light is determined by its <u>wavelength</u>.

87. Answer: c
   The following shows an order from low frequency to high frequency:
   radio, radar, infrared, visible light, ultraviolet, and x-ray.

88. Answer: d
   Pay attention to the word "not."

   Land cost is not related to life cycle costing for a given site, and is therefore the correct answer.

The following are part of life-cycle cost, and are therefore the incorrect answers:
- unscheduled maintenance
- renewal and replacement
- construction cost
- energy costs
- minor repair

89. Answer: If we place a one-candela (candlepower) source at the center of a transparent sphere with a one-<u>meter</u> radius, the amount of luminous energy emanating from one square meter of the surface of the sphere is <u>one lumen (lm) or one lux.</u>

If we place a one-candela (candlepower) source at the center of a transparent sphere with a one-<u>foot</u> radius, the amount of luminous energy emanating from one square foot of the surface of the sphere is <u>one footcandle (fc)</u>.

1 footcandle = 10.76 lux

Note: This formula is easy to understand and memorize. The light density is higher when the spherical surface is closer to the light source.

1 s.m. = 10.76 s.f.

90. Answer: f (none of the above)

Pay attention to the word "not."

All of the following are related to human ability to see an object, and are therefore the incorrect answers:
- size of the object
- familiarity with the object
- lighting
- disability glare
- the observer

91. Answer: c
One of the reasons that the ceiling and upper walls of a room are often painted with light colors is to make the glare from ceiling lights less objectionable. Glare is much more objectionable with a dark background.

Light-colored paints will NOT make the ceiling and walls maintenance free, or easier to clean.

92. Answer: e (None of the above)
Pay attention to the word "not."

All of the following are components of the total daylight factor, and are therefore the incorrect answers:
- sky component
- externally reflected component
- reflected skylight
- reflected groundlight

Internally reflected components include reflected skylight and reflected groundlight.

93. Answer: a
The National Energy Policy Act of 1992 (EPAct) mandates minimum efficacy in lumens per watt and minimum color rendering index for fluorescent lamp types.

The following are **distracters**:
- Illuminating Engineering Society of North America (IESNA) Standard 90.1-2007
- EPA
- USGBC

94. Answer: Fluorescent lamps with efficacies of about 85 lm/W are one of the most efficient light sources available. They convert about <u>25</u> percent of their energy to useful light, <u>35</u> percent of their energy to infrared light, and about <u>40</u> percent of their energy to dissipated heat.

95. Answer: a
Pay attention to the word "not."

Fluorescent is not a type of high-intensity discharge (HID) lamps.

Mercury, metal-halide, and sodium-vapor are types of high-intensity discharge (HID) lamps, and are therefore the incorrect answers.

B. Mock Exam Solution: BS Graphic Vignette Section

1. **Step-by-step solution to the graphic vignette: Mechanical & Electrical Plan**

   1) Open the NCARB graphic program, and find a large blank area.
   2) Since we have all the critical dimensions for the building, we can use the **sketch** tool in the NCARB graphic program to draw a background outline defining the major spaces that we will work on. Use **Sketch > Rectangle** to draw some temporary rectangles to locate the bar joists, and then use **Sketch> Line** to draw the bar joists (figure 4.3). Alternatively you may use the .dwg file provided at our website: http://GreenExamEducation.com/

   3) Determine the **spacing for the recessed fluorescent fixtures:**
      * The vertical distance between the desk level and ceiling = the ceiling height – the desk height = 9'-0" – 3'-0" = 6'-0".
      * The required light level is approximately 50 footcandles measured at desk level.
      * For both the **sides** and **ends** of the 2'x2' lights and the short **ends** of the 2'x4' lights, use the appropriate lighting diagram to determine the spacing. In both the fluorescent fixture 2'x2' and 2'x4' (end) diagrams the line 6'-0" below the ceiling intersects the curved line representing 50 footcandles at 2'-0" from the edge of the recessed fluorescent fixture. This means that we need to place 2'x2' lights and short **ends** of the 2'x4' lights approximately 2'-0" from the walls and 4'-0" apart from one another.
      * For the long **sides** of the 2'x4' lights, use the lighting diagram with the subtitle "Recessed Fluorescent Fixture (2'x4') Side." Here we notice the line 6'-0" below the ceiling intersects the curved line representing 50 footcandles at 3'-0" from the edge of the recessed fluorescent fixture. This means that we need to place the long **sides** of the 2'x4' lights 3'-0" from the walls and 6'-0" apart from one another.

      Note:
      *It is **absolute critical** for ARE candidates to learn how **to read the lighting diagrams**. This is key in passing the vignette of ARE BS division vignette. For the lighting diagrams in the NCARB practice program, the numbers on the left side show the vertical distance from the ceiling, the numbers along the bottom line represent the horizontal distance from the edge of the light fixture, and the curved lines mark the lighting level in footcandles.*

      It is almost impossible to get the EXACT 50 footcandles in each room as required by the NCARB program. Every room will be either over or under lit. Get as close to 50 footcandles as you can, and evenly light each space.

   4) For the Exam Room located at the lower-left-hand corner of the screen, use **Draw > Grid**, and click on two opposite corners of room to draw the grid (figure 4.4). Keep the following in mind when laying out the ceiling grid:
      * Make the ceiling grid symmetrical in order to provide an even lighting level within the room.

- The layout should be oriented with respect to the lights and spacing we discovered in previous steps.

5) **Rotate** and **adjust** the ceiling grids to make it looks symmetrical:
   - If we used the **sketch** tool to draw the background, some elements may overlap. When elements overlap, you may have trouble selecting a particular element. If this happens, keep clicking (without moving the mouse) until the desired element highlights.
   - Click on **rotate** and then click anywhere within the grid to turn the orientation of the grid by 90 degrees.
   - Use the **move, adjust** tool and click anywhere within the grid to shift the cells within the perimeter of the grid rectangle.
   - Use the **move, adjust** tool and click on an edge of the grid rectangle to increase or decrease the length or width of the entire object (figure 4.5).

6) Use **Draw>Recessed Fluorescent Fixture – 2'x2'x6"** to draw 6 lights, and place them approximately 2'-0" from the walls and 4'-0" apart (figure 4.6).

7) Find the square footage of the grid, which is also the square footage of the Exam Room:
   - Click on **id?** then click anywhere within the grid. On the lower left hand corner of the screen, you will see **Grid: 178.89 ft²** (figure 4.7).

   Note: This is an important trick to avoid calculating the room area manually and will save your time in the real exam

   - Since the program states we need to provide one supply diffuser and one return-air grille for every 144 s.f. of floor area (or portion thereof) in each space, we will show two supply diffusers and two return-air grilles for this Exam Room (178.89/144 = 1.24).

8) Use **Draw > Diffuser** to draw two supply diffusers and spread them evenly throughout the room (figure 4.8).

9) Use **Draw > Return-Air Grille** to draw two return-air grilles and spread them evenly. Separate the diffusers and return-air grilles as much as you can. They should be at least 4'-0"apart (figure 4.9).

Note: It is best to have the diffusers and return-air grilles supported by the grid on three sides.

OR
Place the two short edges of the return-air grilles on the grid, and align one long edge along the side of a 2'x2' recessed fluorescent fixture. This is useful for some difficult conditions.

10) Repeat previous steps and draw the grid, supply diffusers, return-air grilles, and lights for the remaining rooms (figure 4.10).

11) Use **Draw > Rigid Duct** to draw the rigid ducts for the supply air and return air. Do NOT forget the short rigid duct for the return air (figure 4.11).

   *Note: Rigid ducts that run **perpendicular** to joists must be within 2'-0" of a steel beam or bearing wall.*

12) Use **Draw > Fire Damper** to draw the fire damper. Click on **rotate** and then on the fire damper symbol. Turn it so that the short "leg" of the fire damper symbol should point **in the direction of air travel** inside the duct (figure 4.12).

13) Use **Draw > Flexible Duct and** draw the flexible ducts to ALL diffusers, even if they overlap or touch the rigid duct. Do NOT miss any diffusers. Flexible duct lengths should not exceed 10'-0" (figure 4.13). When you draw a flexible duct, its length is displayed on the lower left corner of the screen.

   Note: A single flex duct can only connect one supply diffuser. Do NOT use it to connect more than one.

14) Determine the **spacing for the accent light fixtures** in the Waiting Area:
   - For the accent light fixtures, the program requires the light level **between** the fixtures at 5'-0"**above** the floor (or 4'-0" from the ceiling) to be 80 footcandles.
   - Using the lighting diagrams for the accent light fixtures, we notice that the line 4'-0" below the ceiling intersects the curved line representing 80 footcandles intersects at 2'-0" from the edge of the fixture.

     Note: Accent lights are focused on the wall (a vertical surface), NOT the desk (a horizontal surface). The requirement in the program is for 80 footcandles ON the wall BETWEEN fixtures. So you can use the 4'-0" diameter sketch circles to assist you in locating the accent lights; they should intersect AT the wall.

15) Use **zoom** to enlarge in the Waiting Area. Use **Sketch > Circle** to draw some circles with 2'-0"radiuses to assist you in locating the accent light fixtures. The circles should **intersect** AT the south wall of the Waiting Area. You can use **Sketch > Line** to assist you in aligning the centers of the circles. The centers of the circles are the locations of the accent light fixtures. Skip the accent lights at the door to the Reception/Work Area because the door is at least 6'-8" high.

   *Note: For each the accent light fixture at 5'-0"**above** the floor (or 4'-0" from the ceiling):*
   The lighting level is 80 footcandles at the circle perimeter, lower than 80 footcandles outside the circle, and higher than 80 footcandles inside the circle.

16) Because the accent light fixtures are **recessed**, they can NOT overlap the ceiling grid, recessed fluorescent fixtures, supply diffusers, or return-air grilles. If you have to make some adjustment to allow for the recessed accent fixtures you can:

- Delete some of the 2'x2' recessed lights and relocate new ones.
- Add some 2'x4' recessed lights.
- Use **move group** to move the grid, supply diffusers, and return-air grilles to avoid conflicts with accent light fixtures.

Note: Of course, in the real exam, you can draw the circles first and then draw the remaining items to avoid the trouble of moving and adjusting all of the elements in the room.

On the other hand, the previous steps are very good exercise for you to practice the **move group** *and* **move, adjust** *tools in case you do need to use them in the real exam. The above steps show you some tips on using these tools.*

17) Use **Draw > Recessed accent fixture** to draw the accent light fixtures at the center of each of the circles (figure 4.14).

Note: The accent light fixtures are very small, and people tend to miss them. Make sure you remember to draw them.

18) Use **zoom** to show the entire floor plan. This is your final solution (figure 4.15).

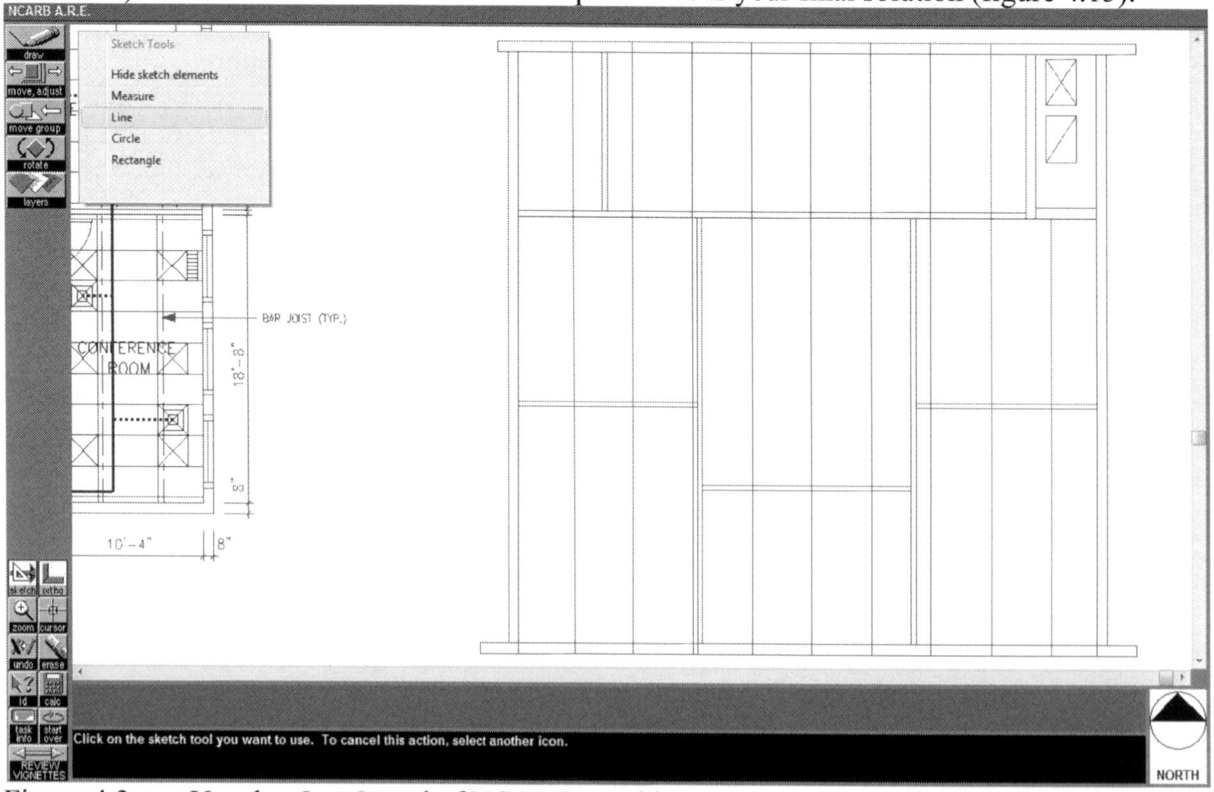

Figure 4.3   Use the **sketch** tool of NCARB graphic program to draw a background outline.

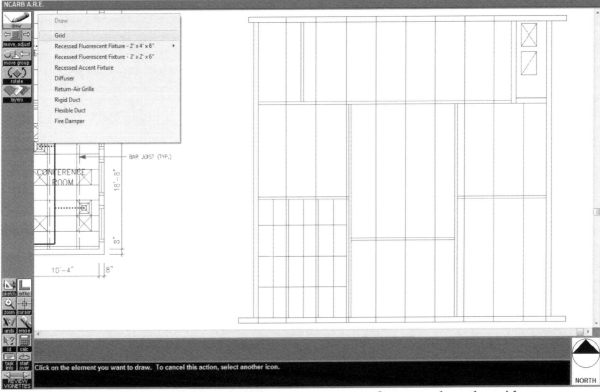

Figure 4.4   Use **Draw > Grid and** click on two corners of room to draw the grid.

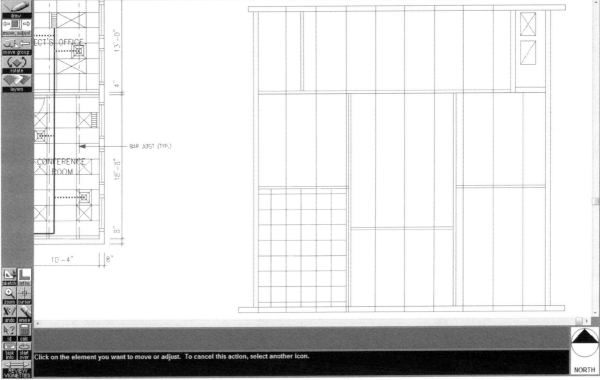

Figure 4.5   **Rotate** and **adjust** the ceiling grids to make it look symmetrical.

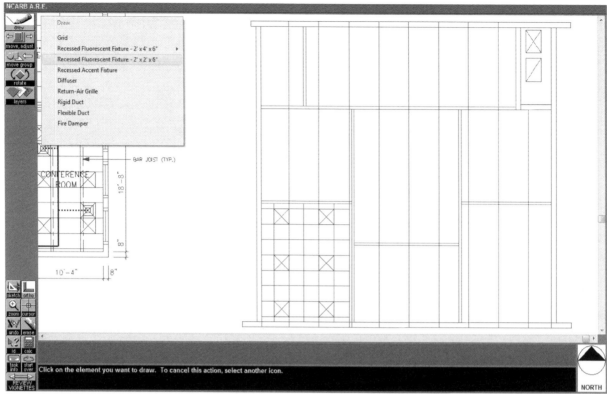

Figure 4.6   Use **Draw > Recessed Fluorescent Fixture – 2'x2'x6"** to draw 6 lights, and place them approximately 2'-0" from the walls and 4'-0" apart from one another.

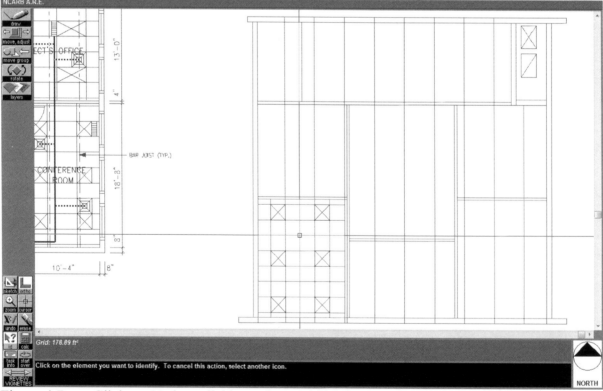

Figure 4.7   Click on **id** then click anywhere within the grid. On the lower left hand corner of the screen, you will see **Grid: 178.89 ft²**.

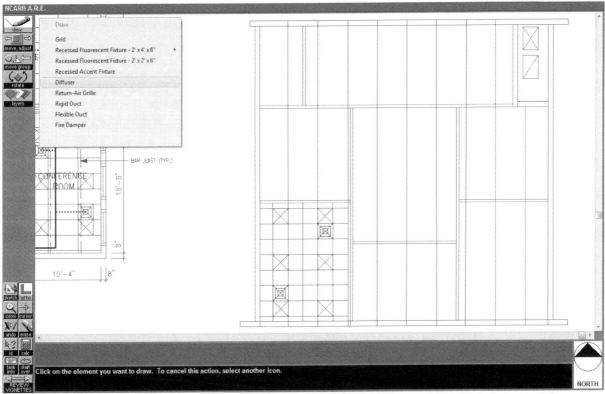

Figure 4.8   Use **Draw > Diffuser** to draw two supply diffusers, and spread them evenly.

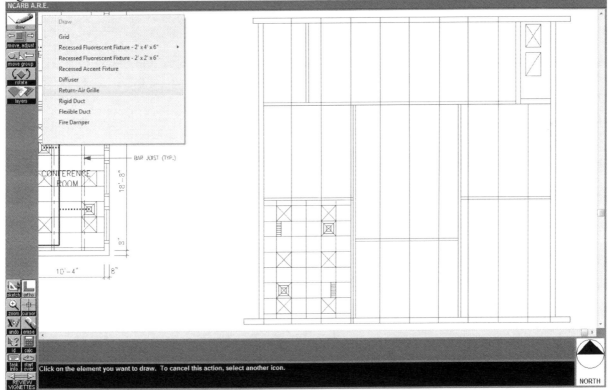

Figure 4.9   Use **Draw > Return Air Grille** to draw two return air grilles, and spread them evenly.

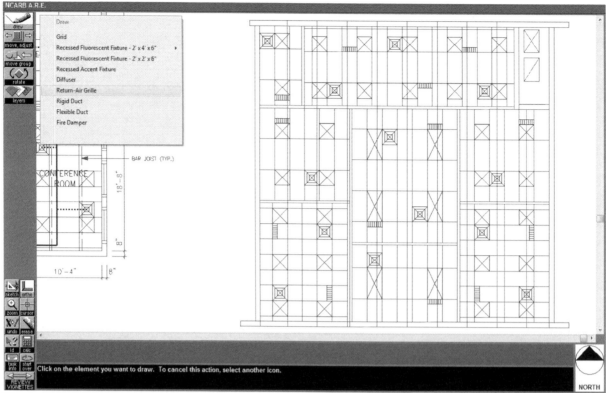

Figure 4.10   Repeat the previous steps and draw the grid, supply diffusers, return-air grilles, and lights for the remaining rooms.

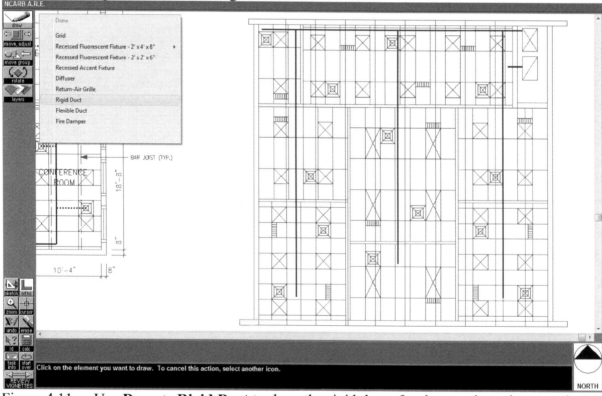

Figure 4.11   Use **Draw > Rigid Duct** to draw the rigid ducts for the supply and return air. Do NOT forget the short rigid duct for the return air.

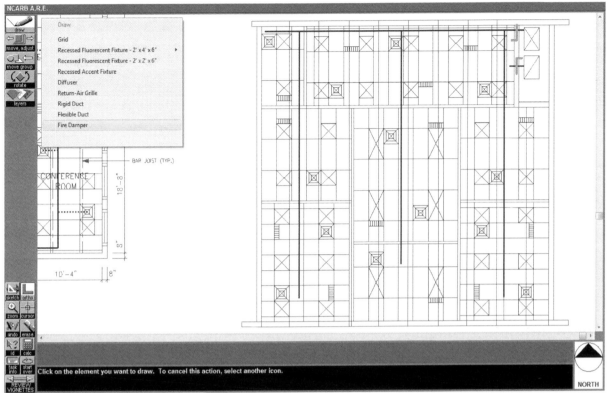

Figure 4.12   The short "leg" of the fire damper symbol should point **in the direction of air travel** inside the duct.

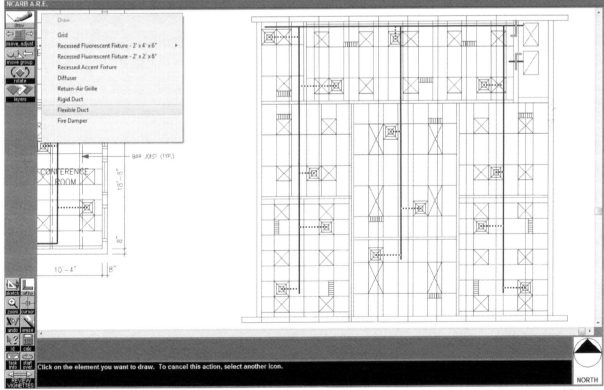

Figure 4.13   Use **Draw > Flexible Duct to** draw the flexible ducts to ALL diffusers, even if they overlap or touch the rigid duct. Flexible duct lengths shall not exceed 10'-0".

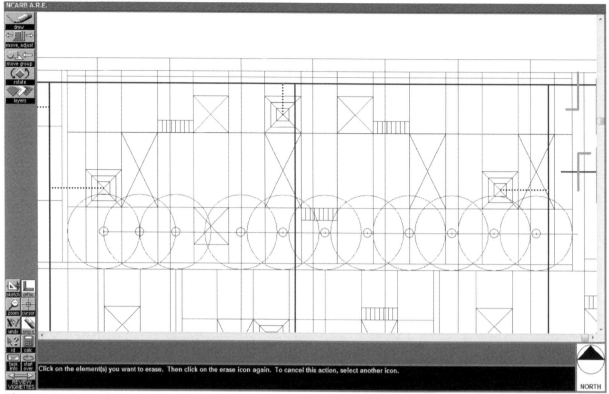

Figure 4.14   The circles should **intersect** AT the south wall of the Waiting Area. The centers of the circles are the locations of the accent light fixtures.

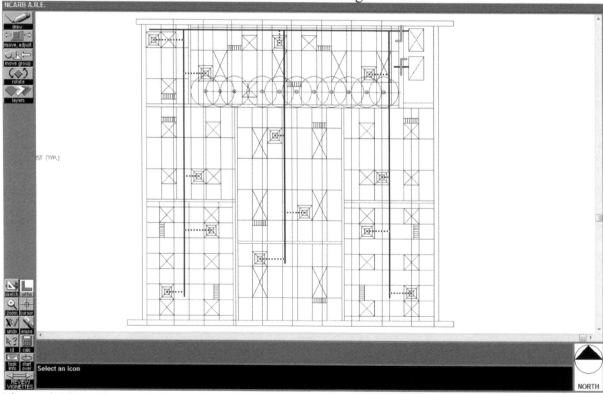

Figure 4.15   Use **zoom** to see the entire plan. This is your final solution.

2. **Notes on graphic vignette traps:**
   Pay attention to the following vignette traps:
   - The ceiling space serves as a return-air plenum. Do NOT forget to connect the return-air plenum to the return riser with **a rigid duct and a fire damper**.
   - Use the "rotate" tool to properly orient all fire dampers: The short "leg" of the fire damper symbol should point **in the direction of air travel** inside the duct.
   - Rigid ducts do **not** fit through joists or between the bottom of joists and the ceiling.
   - Rigid ducts fit under beams and in spaces between joists.
     Note: This requirement is different from the ARE CDS division.
   - Rigid ducts that run **perpendicular** to joists must be within 2'-0" of a beam or bearing wall.
   - Connect each supply diffuser to the rigid supply duct system with flexible duct, even when the diffuser is right under the rigid supply duct.
   - Draw the flexible ducts to ALL diffusers, even if they overlap or touch the rigid duct.
   - Flexible duct lengths shall not exceed 10'-0".
   - Flexible ducts fit through joist webs.
   - A flex duct can only connect one supply diffuser. Do NOT use it to connect more than one.
   - Provide maximum flexibility for furniture layouts.
   - Provide as much separation between the supply air diffusers and return air grille as possible.
   - Provide one supply diffuser and one return-air grille for every 144 s.f. of floor area (or portion thereof) in each space.
   - Do NOT waste time calculating the square footages for each room when you try to layout the diffusers and return-air grilles. Draw the grid in the room first, and then click **id?** as well as the grid. The software will give you the square footage of the room.

Appendixes

A. List of Figures

B. Official Reference Materials Suggested by NCARB

1. General NCARB reference materials for ARE:

Per NCARB, all candidates should become familiar with the latest version of the following codes:

International Code Council, Inc. (ICC, 2006)
International Building Code
International Mechanical Code
International Plumbing Code

National Fire Protection Association (NFPA)
Life Safety Code (NFPA 101)
National Electrical Code (NFPA 70)

National Research Council of Canada
National Building Code of Canada
National Plumbing Code of Canada
National Fire Code of Canada

American Institute of Architects
AIA Documents - 2007

Candidates should be familiar with the Standard on Accessible and Usable Buildings and Facilities (ICC/ANSI A117.1-98)

2. Official NCARB reference materials for the Building Systems (BS) division:

NCARB BS division list of reference and formulas (BSreferences.pdf), a free PDF file available at NCARB website

Architectural Acoustics, Principles & Practice
Cavanaugh, Wilkes
John Wiley & Sons, 1999

Architectural Graphic Standards
Charles G. Ramsey and Harold R. Sleeper
The American Institute of Architects
John Wiley & Sons, latest edition

It is organized roughly per the CSI MasterFormat divisions, including general planning and design data, site work, concrete, masonry, metals, wood, thermal and moisture protection, doors and windows, finishes, specialties, equipment, furnishings, special construction, conveying systems, mechanical, electrical, sports, energy, history preservation, etc.

ASHRAE Fundamentals Handbook
www.ashrae.org
2002-2005

Green Building Materials: A Guide to Product Selection and Specification
Second Edition
Ross Spiegel and Dru Meadows
John Wiley & Sons, 2006

Handbook of Utilities and Services for Buildings: Planning, Design, and Installation
Cyril M. Harris
McGraw-Hill, 1990

Handbook on Safety Code for Elevators and Escalators (A17.1)
CSA 844
American Society of Mechanical Engineers, 2004
www.asme.org

Heating, Cooling, and Lighting: Design Methods for Architects
Norbert Lechner
John Wiley & Sons, latest edition

Inside Out: Design Procedures for Passive Environmental Design
G. Z. Brown et al.
John Wiley & Sons, 1982

Mechanical & Electrical Equipment for Buildings (MEEB)
Benjamin Stein and John S. Reynolds
John Wiley& Sons, latest edition

Mechanical & Electrical Systems for Historic Buildings
Gersil Newmark Kay
McGraw-Hill, 1992

Passive Solar Design and Construction Handbook
Steven Winter Associates and Michael J. Crosbie, Editors
John Wiley & Sons, 1997

Simplified Design for Building Fire Safety
James Patterson
John Wiley & Sons, 1993

Sun, Wind, and Light: Architectural Design Strategies,
Second Edition
G. Z. Brown and Mark DeKay
John Wiley & Sons, 2000

Understanding Infrastructure: A Guide for Architects and Planners
George Rainer
John Wiley & Sons, 1990

C. Other reference materials

Chen, Gang. *Building Construction: Project Management, Construction Administration, Drawings, Specs, Detailing Tips, Schedules, Checklists, and Secrets Others Don't Tell You (Architectural Practice Simplified, 2nd edition).* ArchiteG, Inc., A good introduction to the architectural practice and construction documents and service, including discussions of MasterSpec format and specification sections.

Chen, Gang. *LEED GA Exam Guide: A Must-Have for the LEED Green Associate Exam: Comprehensive Study Materials, Sample Questions, Mock Exam, Green Building LEED Certification, and Sustainability.* ArchiteG, Inc., latest edition. A good introduction to green buildings and the LEED building rating system.

Ching, Francis. *Architecture: Form, Space, & Order.* Wiley, latest edition. It is one of the best architectural books that you can have. I still flip through it every now and then. It is a great book for inspiration.

Ching, Francis. Steven R. Winkel, FAIA, PE. *Building Codes Illustrated: A Guide to Understanding the International Building Code.* Wiley, latest edition. A valuable interpretive guide with many useful line drawings. A great timesaver.

Frampton, Kenneth. *Modern Architecture: A Critical History.* Thames and Hudson, London, latest edition. A valuable resource for architectural history.

Jarzombek, Mark M. (Author), Vikramaditya Prakash (Author), Francis D. K. Ching (Editor). *A Global History of Architecture.* Wiley, latest edition. A valuable and comprehensive resource for architectural history with 1000 b & w photos, 50 color photos, and 1500 b & w illustrations. It doesn't limit the topic on a Western perspective, but rather through a global vision.

Trachtenberg, Marvin and Isabelle Hyman. *Architecture: From Pre-history to Post-Modernism.* Prentice Hall, Englewood Cliffs, NJ. Latest edition. A valuable and comprehensive resource for architectural history.

D. Definition of "Architect" and Other Important Information About Architects and the Profession of Architecture

Architects, Except Landscape and Naval

- <u>Nature of the Work</u>
- <u>Training, Other Qualifications, and Advancement</u>
- <u>Employment</u>
- <u>Job Outlook</u>
- <u>Projections Data</u>
- <u>Earnings</u>
- <u>OES Data</u>
- <u>Related Occupations</u>
- <u>Sources of Additional Information</u>

Significant Points

- About one in five architects are self-employed—more than two times the proportion for all other occupations.
- Licensing requirements include a professional degree in architecture, at least three years of practical work training, and passing all divisions of the Architect Registration Examination.
- Architecture graduates may face competition, especially for jobs in the most prestigious firms.

Nature of the Work

People need places in which to live, work, play, learn, worship, meet, govern, shop, and eat. These places may be private or public; indoors or out; rooms, single buildings or complexes, and architects are the individuals who design them. Architects are licensed professionals trained in the art and science of building design who develop the concepts for structures and turn those concepts into images and plans.

Architects create the overall aesthetic and look of buildings and other structures, but the design of a building involves far more than its appearance. Buildings must also be functional, safe, economical, and must suit the needs of the people who use them. Architects consider all these factors when they design buildings and other structures.

Architects may be involved in all phases of a construction project, from the initial discussion with the client through the entire construction process. Their duties require specific skills—designing, engineering, managing, supervising, and communicating with clients and builders. Architects spend a great deal of time explaining their ideas to clients, construction contractors, and others. Successful architects must be able to communicate their unique vision persuasively.

The architect and client discuss the objectives, requirements, and budget of a project. In some cases, architects provide various pre-design services such as conducting feasibility and environmental impact studies, selecting a site, preparing cost analysis and land-use studies, or specifying the requirements the design must meet. For example, they may determine space requirements by researching the numbers and types of potential users of a building. The architect then prepares drawings and a report presenting ideas for the client to review.

After discussing and agreeing on the initial proposal, architects develop final construction plans that show the building's appearance and details for its construction. Accompanying these plans are drawings of the structural system; air-conditioning, heating, and ventilating systems; electrical systems; communications systems; plumbing; and, possibly, site and landscape plans. The plans also specify the building materials and, in some cases, the interior furnishings. In developing designs, architects follow building codes, zoning laws, fire regulations, and other ordinances, such as those requiring easy access by people who are disabled. Computer-aided design and drafting (CADD) and Building Information Modeling (BIM) technology has replaced traditional paper and pencil as the most common method for creating design and construction drawings. Continual revision of plans on the basis of client needs and budget constraints is often necessary.

Architects may also assist clients in obtaining construction bids, selecting contractors, and negotiating construction contracts. As construction proceeds, they may visit building sites to make sure that contractors follow the design, adhere to the schedule, use the specified materials, and meet work quality standards. The job is not complete until all construction is finished, required tests are conducted, and construction costs are paid. Sometimes, architects also provide post-construction services, such as facilities management. They advise on energy efficiency measures, evaluate how well the building design adapts to the needs of occupants, and make necessary improvements.

Often working with engineers, urban planners, interior designers, landscape architects, and other professionals, architects in fact spend a great deal of their time coordinating information from, and the work of, other professionals engaged in the same project.

They design a wide variety of buildings, such as office and apartment buildings, schools, churches, factories, hospitals, houses, and airport terminals. They also design complexes such as urban centers, college campuses, industrial parks, and entire communities.
Architects sometimes specialize in one phase of work. Some specialize in the design of one type of building—for example, hospitals, schools, or housing. Others focus on planning and pre-design services or construction management, and do minimal design work.

Work environment. Usually working in a comfortable environment, architects spend most of their time in offices consulting with clients, developing reports and drawings, and working with other architects and engineers. However, they often visit construction sites to review the progress of projects. Although most architects work approximately 40 hours per week, they often have to work nights and weekends to meet deadlines.

Training, Other Qualifications, and Advancement

There are three main steps in becoming an architect. First is the attainment of a professional degree in architecture. Second is work experience through an internship, and third is licensure through the passing of the Architect Registration Exams.

Education and training. In most states, the professional degree in architecture must be from one of the 114 schools of architecture that have degree programs accredited by the National Architectural Accrediting Board. However, state architectural registration boards set their own standards, so graduation from a non-accredited program may meet the educational requirement for licensing in a few states.

Three types of professional degrees in architecture are available: a five year bachelor's degree, which is most common and is intended for students with no previous architectural training; a two year master's degree for students with an undergraduate degree in architecture or a related area; and a three or four year master's degree for students with a degree in another discipline.

The choice of degree depends on preference and educational background. Prospective architecture students should consider the options before committing to a program. For example, although the five-year bachelor of architecture offers the fastest route to the professional degree, courses are specialized, and if the student does not complete the program, transferring to a program in another discipline may be difficult. A typical program includes courses in architectural history and theory, building design with an emphasis on CADD, structures, technology, construction methods, professional practice, math, physical sciences, and liberal arts. Central to most architectural programs is the design studio, where students apply the skills and concepts learned in the classroom, creating drawings and three-dimensional models of their designs.

Many schools of architecture also offer post-professional degrees for those who already have a bachelor's or master's degree in architecture or other areas. Although graduate education beyond the professional degree is not required for practicing architects, it may be required for research, teaching, and certain specialties.

All state architectural registration boards require architecture graduates to complete a training period—usually at least three years—before they may sit for the licensing exam. Every state, with the exception of Arizona, has adopted the training standards established by the Intern Development Program, a branch of the American Institute of Architects and the National Council of Architectural Registration Boards (NCARB). These standards stipulate broad training under the supervision of a licensed architect. Most new graduates complete their training period by working as interns in architectural firms. Some states allow a portion of the training to occur in the offices of related professionals, such as engineers or general contractors. Architecture students who complete internships while still in school can count some of that time toward the three-year training period.

Interns in architectural firms may assist in the design of one part of a project, help prepare architectural documents or drawings, build models, or prepare construction drawings on

CADD. Interns also may research building codes and materials or write specifications for building materials, installation criteria, the quality of finishes, and other related details.

Licensure. All states and the District of Columbia require individuals to be licensed (registered) before they may call themselves architects and contract to provide architectural services. During the time between graduation and becoming licensed, architecture school graduates generally work in the field under the supervision of a licensed architect who takes legal responsibility for all work. Licensing requirements include a professional degree in architecture, a period of practical training or internship, and a passing score on all divisions of the Architect Registration Examination. The examination is broken into seven divisions consisting of multiple choice and/or graphic vignettes. The eligibility period for completion of all divisions is five years from the date of passing your first exam.

Most states also require some form of continuing education to maintain a license, and many others are expected to adopt mandatory continuing education. Requirements vary by state but usually involve the completion of a certain number of credits annually or biennially through workshops, formal university classes, conferences, self-study courses, or other sources.

Other qualifications. Architects must be able to communicate their ideas visually to their clients. Artistic and drawing ability is helpful, but not essential, to such communication. More important are a visual orientation and the ability to understand spatial relationships. Other important qualities for anyone interested in becoming an architect are creativity and the ability to work independently and as part of a team. Computer skills are also required for writing specifications, for two and three dimensional drafting using CADD programs, and for financial management.

Certification and advancement. A growing number of architects voluntarily seek certification by the National Council of Architectural Registration Boards. Certification is awarded after independent verification of the candidate's educational transcripts, employment record, and professional references. Certification can make it easier to become licensed across states. In fact, it is the primary requirement for reciprocity of licensing among state boards that are NCARB members. In 2007, approximately one-third of all licensed architects had this certification.

After becoming licensed and gaining experience, architects take on increasingly responsible duties, eventually managing entire projects. In large firms, architects may advance to supervisory or managerial positions. Some architects become partners in established firms, while others set up their own practices. Some graduates with degrees in architecture also enter related fields, such as graphic, interior, industrial design, urban planning, real estate development, civil engineering, or construction management.

Employment

Architects held about 132,000 jobs in 2006. Approximately seven out of ten jobs were in the architectural, engineering, and related services industry—mostly in architectural firms with fewer than five workers. A small number worked for residential and nonresidential building construction firms and for government agencies responsible for housing, community planning, or construction of government buildings, such as the U.S. Departments of Defense and Interior, and the General Services Administration. About one in five architects are self-employed.

Job Outlook

Employment of architects is expected to grow faster than the average for all occupations through 2016. Keen competition is expected for positions at the most prestigious firms, and opportunities will be best for those architects who are able to distinguish themselves with their creativity.

Employment change. Employment of architects is expected to grow by 18 percent between 2006 and 2016, which is faster than the average for all occupations. Employment of architects is strongly tied to the activity of the construction industry. Strong growth is expected to come from nonresidential construction as demand for commercial space increases. Residential construction, buoyed by low interest rates, is also expected to grow as more people become homeowners. If interest rates rise significantly, home building may fall off, but residential construction makes up only a small part of architects' work.

Current demographic trends also support an increase in demand for architects. As the population of Sunbelt States continues to grow, the people living there will need new places to live and work. As the population continues to live longer and baby-boomers begin to retire, there will be a need for more healthcare facilities, nursing homes, and retirement communities. In education, buildings at all levels are getting older and class sizes are getting larger. This will require many school districts and universities to build new facilities and renovate existing ones.

In recent years, some architecture firms have outsourced the drafting of construction documents and basic design for large-scale commercial and residential projects to architecture firms overseas. This trend is expected to continue and may have a negative impact on employment growth for lower level architects and interns who would normally gain experience by producing these drawings.

Job prospects. Besides employment growth, additional job openings will arise from the need to replace the many architects who are nearing retirement, and others who transfer to other occupations or stop working for other reasons. Internship opportunities for new architectural students are expected to be good over the next decade, but more students are graduating with architectural degrees and some competition for entry-level jobs can be anticipated. Competition will be especially keen for jobs at the most prestigious architectural firms as prospective architects try to build their reputation. Prospective architects who have had internships while in school will have an advantage in obtaining intern positions after graduation. Opportunities will be best for those architects that are able to distinguish themselves from others with their creativity.

Prospects will also be favorable for architects with knowledge of "green" design. Green design, also known as sustainable design, emphasizes energy efficiency, renewable resources such as energy and water, waste reduction, and environmentally friendly design, specifications, and materials. Rising energy costs and increased concern about the environment has led to many new buildings being built green.

Some types of construction are sensitive to cyclical changes in the economy. Architects seeking design projects for office and retail construction will face especially strong competition for jobs or clients during recessions, and layoffs may ensue in less successful firms. Those involved in the design of institutional buildings, such as schools, hospitals, nursing homes, and correctional facilities, will be less affected by fluctuations in the economy. Residential construction makes up a small portion of work for architects, so major changes in the housing market would not be as significant as fluctuations in the nonresidential market.

Despite good overall job opportunities, some architects may not fare as well as others. The profession is geographically sensitive, and some parts of the Nation may have fewer new building projects. Also, many firms specialize in specific buildings, such as hospitals or office towers, and demand for these buildings may vary by region. Architects may find it increasingly necessary to gain reciprocity in order to compete for the best jobs and projects in other states.

Projections Data

Projections data from the National Employment Matrix

Occupational title	SOC Code	Employment, 2006	Projected employment, 2016	Change, 2006-16		Detailed statistics
				Number	Percent	
Architects, except landscape and naval	17-1011	132,000	155,000	23,000	18	PDF zipped XLS

NOTE: Data in this table are rounded. See the discussion of the employment projections table in the *Handbook* introductory chapter on *Occupational Information Included in the Handbook*.

Earnings

Median annual earnings of wage-and-salary architects were $64,150 in May 2006. The middle 50 percent earned between $49,780 and $83,450. The lowest 10 percent earned less than $39,420, and the highest 10 percent earned more than $104,970. Those just starting their internships can expect to earn considerably less.

Earnings of partners in established architectural firms may fluctuate because of changing business conditions. Some architects may have difficulty establishing their own practices and may go through a period when their expenses are greater than their income, requiring substantial financial resources.

Many firms pay tuition and fees toward continuing education requirements for their employees.

For the latest wage information:
The above wage data is from the Occupational Employment Statistics (OES) survey program, unless otherwise noted. For the latest national, state, and local earnings data, visit the following pages:
Architects, except landscape and naval

Related Occupations
Architects design buildings and related structures. Construction managers, like architects, also plan and coordinate activities concerned with the construction and maintenance of buildings and facilities. Others who engage in similar work are landscape architects, civil engineers, urban and regional planners, and designers, including interior designers, commercial and industrial designers, and graphic designers.

Sources of Additional Information

Disclaimer:
Links to non-BLS Internet sites are provided for your convenience and do not constitute an endorsement.

Information about education and careers in architecture can be obtained from:
- The American Institute of Architects, 1735 New York Ave. NW., Washington, DC 20006. Internet: http://www.aia.org
- Intern Development Program, National Council of Architectural Registration Boards, Suite 1100K, 1801 K St. NW., Washington, D.C. 20006.
  Internet: http://www.ncarb.org
  OOH ONET Codes 17-1011.00"

Quoted from: Bureau of Labor Statistics, U.S. Department of Labor, Occupational Outlook Handbook, 2008-09 Edition, Architects, Except Landscape and Naval, on the Internet at **http://www.bls.gov/oco/ocos038.htm** (visited November 30, 2008).
Last Modified Date: December 18, 2007

Note: Please check the website above for the latest information.

E. AIA Compensation Survey

Every three years, AIA publishes a Compensation Survey for various positions at architectural firms across the country. It is a good idea to find out the salary before you make the final decision to become an architect. If you are already an architect, it is also a good idea to determine if you are underpaid or overpaid.

See following link for an article on the 2011 AIA Compensation Survey:

http://www.architectmagazine.com/architecture/aia-survey-reports-marginal-increases-in-compensation.aspx

You can purchase the complete 2011 AIA Compensation Survey at AIA web store at the following link:

http://aiastore.hostedbywebstore.com/AIA-Compensation-Survey-2011-Report/dp/B0058OE1U8

F. So ... You would Like to Study Architecture

To study architecture, you need to learn how to draft, how to understand and organize spaces and the interactions between interior and exterior spaces, how to do design, and how to communicate effectively. You also need to understand the history of architecture.

As an architect, a leader for a team of various design professionals, you not only need to know architecture, but also need to understand enough of your consultants' work to be able to coordinate with them. Your consultants include soils and civil engineers, landscape architects, structural, electrical, mechanical, and plumbing engineers, interior designers, sign consultants, etc.

There are two major career paths for you in architecture: practice as an architect or teach in college or university. The earlier you determine which path you are going to take, the more likely you will be successful at an early age. Some famous and well-respected architects, like my USC alumnus Frank Gehry, have combined the two paths successfully. They teach at the universities and have their own architectural practice. Even as a college or university professor, people respect you more if you have actual working experience and have some built projects. If you only teach in colleges or universities but have no actual working experience and have no built projects, people will consider you as a "paper" architect, and they are not likely to take you seriously, because they will think you probably do not know how to put a real building together.

In the United States, if you want to practice architecture, you need to obtain an architect's license. It requires a combination of passing scores on the Architectural Registration Exam (ARE) and eight years of education and/or qualified working experience, including at least one year of working experience in the United States. Your working experience needs to be under the supervision of a licensed architect to be counted as qualified working experience for your architect's license.

If you work for a landscape architect or civil engineer or structural engineer, some states' architectural licensing boards will count your experience at a discounted rate for the qualification of your architect's license. For example, two years of experience working for a civil engineer may be counted as one year of qualified experience for your architect's license. Contact your state's architectural licensing board for specific licensing requirements.

If you want to teach in colleges or universities, you probably want to obtain a master's degree or a Ph.D. It is not very common for people in the architectural field to have a Ph.D. One reason is that there are few Ph.D. programs for architecture. Another reason is that architecture is considered a profession and requires a license. Many people think an architect's license is more important than a Ph.D. degree. In many states, you need to have an architect's license to even use the title "architect," or the terms "architectural" or "architecture" to advertise your service. You cannot call yourself an architect if you do not have an architect's license, even if you have a Ph.D. in architecture. Violation of these rules brings punishment.

To become a tenured professor, you need to have a certain number of publications and pass the evaluation for the tenure position. Publications are very important for tenure track positions. Some people say it is "publish or perish" for the tenured track positions in universities and colleges.

The American Institute of Architects (AIA) is the national organization for the architectural profession. Membership is voluntary. There are different levels of AIA membership. Only licensed architects can be (full) AIA members. If you are an architectural student or an intern but not a licensed architect yet, you can join as an associate AIA member. Contact AIA for detailed information.

The National Council of Architectural Registration Boards (NCARB) is a nonprofit federation of architectural licensing boards. It has some very useful programs, such as IDP, to assist you in obtaining your architect's license. Contact NCARB for detailed information.

Back Page Promotion

You may be interested in some other books written by Gang Chen:

A. **ARE Mock Exam series. See the following link:**
   http://www.GreenExamEducation.com

B. **LEED Exam Guides series. See the following link:**
   http://www.GreenExamEducation.com

C. ***Building Construction:*** *Project Management, Construction Administration, Drawings, Specs, Detailing Tips, Schedules, Checklists, and Secrets Others Don't Tell You (Architectural Practice Simplified, 2nd edition)*
   http://www.ArchiteG.com

D. ***Planting Design Illustrated***
   http://outskirtspress.com/agent.php?key=11011&page=GangChen

ARE Mock Exam Series

Published ARE books (One Mock Exam book for each ARE division, plus California Supplemental Mock Exam):
Programming, Planning & Practice (PPP) ARE Mock Exam (Architect Registration Exam): ARE Overview, Exam Prep Tips, Multiple-Choice Questions and Graphic Vignettes, Solutions and Explanations. **ISBN-13:** 9781612650067

Site Planning & Design ARE Mock Exam (SPD of Architect Registration Exam): ARE Overview, Exam Prep Tips, Multiple-Choice Questions and Graphic Vignettes, Solutions and Explanations. **ISBN-13:** 9781612650111

Building Design and Construction Systems (BDCS) ARE Mock Exam (Architect Registration Exam): ARE Overview, Exam Prep Tips, Multiple-Choice Questions and Graphic Vignettes, Solutions and Explanations. **ISBN-13:** 9781612650029

Schematic Design (SD) ARE Mock Exam (Architect Registration Exam): ARE Overview, Exam Prep Tips, Graphic Vignettes, Solutions and Explanations
ISBN: 9781612650050

Structural Systems ARE Mock Exam (SS of Architect Registration Exam): ARE Overview, Exam Prep Tips, Multiple-Choice Questions and Graphic Vignettes, Solutions and Explanations. **ISBN**: 9781612650012

Building Systems (BS) ARE Mock Exam (Architect Registration Exam): ARE Overview, Exam Prep Tips, Multiple-Choice Questions and Graphic Vignettes, Solutions and Explanations. **ISBN-13**: 9781612650036

Construction Documents and Service (CDS) Are Mock Exam (Architect Registration Exam): ARE Overview, Exam Prep Tips, Multiple-Choice Questions and Graphic Vignettes, Solutions and Explanations. **ISBN-13:** 9781612650005

Mock California Supplemental Exam (CSE of Architect Registration Exam): CSE Overview, Exam Prep Tips, General Section and Project Scenario Section, Questions, Solutions and Explanations. **ISBN**: 9781612650159

Upcoming ARE books:
Other books in the ARE Mock Exam Series are being produced. Our goal is to produce one mock exam book PLUS one guidebook for each of the ARE exam divisions.

See the following link for the latest information:
http://www.GreenExamEducation.com

LEED Exam Guides series*: Comprehensive Study Materials, Sample Questions, Mock Exam, Building LEED Certification and Going Green**

LEED (Leadership in Energy and Environmental Design) is the most important trend of development, and it is revolutionizing the construction industry. It has gained tremendous momentum and has a profound impact on our environment.

From LEED Exam Guides series, you will learn how to

1. Pass the LEED Green Associate Exam and various LEED AP + exams (each book will help you with a specific LEED exam).

2. Register and certify a building for LEED certification.

3. Understand the intent for each LEED prerequisite and credit.

4. Calculate points for a LEED credit.

5. Identify the responsible party for each prerequisite and credit.

6. Earn extra credit (exemplary performance) for LEED.

7. Implement the local codes and building standards for prerequisites and credit.

8. Receive points for categories not yet clearly defined by USGBC.

There is currently NO official book on the LEED Green Associate Exam, and most of the existing books on LEED and LEED AP are too expensive and too complicated to be practical and helpful. The pocket guides in LEED Exam Guides series fill in the blanks, demystify LEED, and uncover the tips, codes, and jargon for LEED as well as the true meaning of "going green." They will set up a solid foundation and fundamental framework of LEED for you. Each book in the LEED Exam Guides series covers every aspect of one or more specific LEED rating system(s) in plain and concise language and makes this information understandable to all people.

These pocket guides are small and easy to carry around. You can read them whenever you have a few extra minutes. They are indispensable books for all people—administrators; developers; contractors; architects; landscape architects; civil, mechanical, electrical, and plumbing engineers; interns; drafters; designers; and other design professionals.

Why is the LEED Exam Guides series needed?

A number of books are available that you can use to prepare for the LEED exams:

1. *USGBC Reference Guides*. You need to select the correct version of the *Reference Guide* for your exam.

    The *USGBC Reference Guides* are comprehensive, but they give too much information. For example, *The LEED 2009 Reference Guide for Green Building Design and Construction (BD&C)* has about 700 oversized pages. Many of the calculations in the books are too detailed for the exam. They are also expensive (approximately $200 each, so most people may not buy them for their personal use, but instead, will seek to share an office copy).

    It is good to read a reference guide from cover to cover if you have the time. The problem is not too many people have time to read the whole reference guide. Even if you do read the whole guide, you may not remember the important issues to pass the LEED exam. You need to reread the material several times before you can remember much of it.

    Reading the reference guide from cover to cover without a guidebook is a difficult and inefficient way of preparing for the LEED AP Exam, because you do NOT know what USGBC and GBCI are looking for in the exam.

2. The USGBC workshops and related handouts are concise, but they do not cover extra credits (exemplary performance). The workshops are expensive, costing approximately $450 each.

3. Various books published by a third party are available on Amazon, bn.com and books.google.com. However, most of them are not very helpful.

    There are many books on LEED, but not all are useful.

    LEED Exam Guides series will fill in the blanks and become a valuable, reliable source:

    a. They will give you more information for your money. Each of the books in the LEED Exam Guides series has more information than the related USGBC workshops.

    b. They are exam-oriented and more effective than the USGBC reference guides.

    c. They are better than most, if not all, of the other third-party books. They give you comprehensive study materials, sample questions and answers, mock exams and answers, and critical information on building LEED certification and going green. Other third-party books only give you a fraction of the information.

    d. They are comprehensive yet concise. They are small and easy to carry around. You can read them whenever you have a few extra minutes.

    e. They are great timesavers. I have highlighted the important information that you need to understand and MEMORIZE. I also make some acronyms and short sentences to help you easily remember the credit names.

It should take you about 1 or 2 weeks of full-time study to pass each of the LEED exams. I have met people who have spent 40 hours to study and passed the exams.

You can find sample texts and other information on the LEED Exam Guides series in customer discussion sections under each of my book's listing on Amazon, bn.com and books.google.com.

What others are saying about *LEED GA Exam Guide* (Book 2, LEED Exam Guide series):

"Finally! A comprehensive study tool for LEED GA Prep!

"I took the 1-day Green LEED GA course and walked away with a power point binder printed in very small print—which was missing MUCH of the required information (although I didn't know it at the time). I studied my little heart out and took the test, only to fail it by 1 point. Turns out I did NOT study all the material I needed to in order to pass the test. I found this book, read it, marked it up, retook the test, and passed it with a 95%. Look, we all know the LEED GA exam is new and the resources for study are VERY limited. This one is the VERY best out there right now. I highly recommend it."
—ConsultantVA

"Complete overview for the LEED GA exam

"I studied this book for about 3 days and passed the exam … if you are truly interested in learning about the LEED system and green building design, this is a great place to start."
—K.A. Evans

"A Wonderful Guide for the LEED GA Exam

"After deciding to take the LEED Green Associate exam, I started to look for the best possible study materials and resources. From what I thought would be a relatively easy task, it turned into a tedious endeavor. I realized that there are vast amounts of third-party guides and handbooks. Since the official sites offer little to no help, it became clear to me that my best chance to succeed and pass this exam would be to find the most comprehensive study guide that would not only teach me the topics, but would also give me a great background and understanding of what LEED actually is. Once I stumbled upon Mr. Chen's book, all my needs were answered. This is a great study guide that will give the reader the most complete view of the LEED exam and all that it entails.

"The book is written in an easy-to-understand language and brings up great examples, tying the material to the real world. The information is presented in a coherent and logical way, which optimizes the learning process and does not go into details that will not be needed for the LEED Green Associate Exam, as many other guides do. This book stays dead on topic and keeps the reader interested in the material.

"I highly recommend this book to anyone that is considering the LEED Green Associate Exam. I learned a great deal from this guide, and I am feeling very confident about my chances for passing my upcoming exam."
—Pavel Geystrin

"Easy to read, easy to understand

"I have read through the book once and found it to be the perfect study guide for me. The author does a great job of helping you get into the right frame of mind for the content of the exam. I had started by studying the Green Building Design and Construction reference guide for LEED projects produced by the USGBC. That was the wrong approach, simply too much information with very little retention. At 636 pages in textbook format, it would have been a daunting task to get through it. Gang Chen breaks down the points, helping to minimize the amount of information but maximizing the content I was able to absorb. I plan on going through the book a few more times, and I now believe I have the right information to pass the LEED Green Associate Exam."
—**Brian Hochstein**

"All in one—LEED GA prep material

"Since the LEED Green Associate exam is a newer addition by USGBC, there is not much information regarding study material for this exam. When I started looking around for material, I got really confused about what material I should buy. This LEED GA guide by Gang Chen is an answer to all my worries! It is a very precise book with lots of information, like how to approach the exam, what to study and what to skip, links to online material, and tips and tricks for passing the exam. It is like the 'one stop shop' for the LEED Green Associate Exam. I think this book can also be a good reference guide for green building professionals. A must-have!"
—**SwatiD**

"An ESSENTIAL LEED GA Exam Reference Guide

"This book is an invaluable tool in preparation for the LEED Green Associate (GA) Exam. As a practicing professional in the consulting realm, I found this book to be all-inclusive of the preparatory material needed for sitting the exam. The information provides clarity to the fundamental and advanced concepts of what LEED aims to achieve. A tremendous benefit is the connectivity of the concepts with real-world applications.

"The author, Gang Chen, provides a vast amount of knowledge in a very clear, concise, and logical media. For those that have not picked up a textbook in a while, it is very manageable to extract the needed information from this book. If you are taking the exam, do yourself a favor and purchase a copy of this great guide. Applicable fields: Civil Engineering, Architectural Design, MEP, and General Land Development."
—**Edwin L. Tamang**

Note: Other books in the **LEED Exam Guides series** are in the process of being produced. At least **one book will eventually be produced for each of the LEED exams.** The series include:

LEED v4 Green Associate Exam Guide (LEED GA): *Comprehensive Study Materials, Sample Questions, Mock Exam, Green Building LEED Certification, and Sustainability*, LEED Exam Guide series, ArchiteG.com. Latest Edition.

LEED GA MOCK EXAMS (LEED v4): *Questions, Answers, and Explanations: A Must-Have for the LEED Green Associate Exam, Green Building LEED Certification, and Sustainability*, LEED Exam Guide series, ArchiteG.com. Latest Edition

LEED v4 BD&C EXAM GUIDE: *A Must-Have for the LEED AP BD+C Exam: Comprehensive Study Materials, Sample Questions, Mock Exam, Green Building Design and Construction, LEED Certification, and Sustainability*, LEED Exam Guide series, ArchiteG.com. Latest Edition.

LEED v4 BD&C MOCK EXAMS: *Questions, Answers, and Explanations: A Must-Have for the LEED AP BD+C Exam, Green Building LEED Certification, and Sustainability*, LEED Exam Guide series, ArchiteG.com. Latest Edition.

LEED ID&C Exam Guide: *A Must-Have for the LEED AP ID+C Exam: Study Materials, Sample Questions, Green Interior Design and Construction, Green Building LEED Certification, and Sustainability*, LEED Exam Guide series, ArchiteG.com. Latest Edition.

LEED ID&C Mock Exam: *Questions, Answers, and Explanations: A Must-Have for the LEED AP ID+C Exam, Green Interior Design and Construction, Green Building LEED Certification, and Sustainability*, LEED Exam Guide series, ArchiteG.com. Latest Edition.

LEED O&M MOCK EXAMS: *Questions, Answers, and Explanations: A Must-Have for the LEED O&M Exam, Green Building LEED Certification, and Sustainability*, LEED Exam Guide series, ArchiteG.com. Latest Edition.

LEED O&M EXAM GUIDE: *A Must-Have for the LEED AP O+M Exam: Comprehensive Study Materials, Sample Questions, Mock Exam, Green Building Operations and Maintenance, LEED Certification, and Sustainability*, LEED Exam Guide series, ArchiteG.com. Latest Edition.

LEED HOMES EXAM GUIDE: *A Must-Have for the LEED AP Homes Exam: Comprehensive Study Materials, Sample Questions, Mock Exam, Green Building LEED Certification, and Sustainability*, LEED Exam Guide series, ArchiteG.com. Latest Edition.

LEED ND EXAM GUIDE: *A Must-Have for the LEED AP Neighborhood Development Exam: Comprehensive Study Materials, Sample Questions, Mock Exam, Green Building LEED Certification, and Sustainability*, LEED Exam Guide series, ArchiteG.com. Latest Edition.

How to order these books:
You can order the books listed above at:
http://www.GreenExamEducation.com

OR
http://www.ArchiteG.com

Building Construction

Project Management, Construction Administration, Drawings, Specs, Detailing Tips, Schedules, Checklists, and Secrets Others Don't Tell You (Architectural Practice Simplified, 2ⁿᵈ edition)

Learn the Tips, Become One of Those Who Know Building Construction and Architectural Practice, and Thrive!

For architectural practice and building design and construction industry, there are two kinds of people: those who know, and those who don't. The tips of building design and construction and project management have been undercover—until now.

Most of the existing books on building construction and architectural practice are too expensive, too complicated, and too long to be practical and helpful. This book simplifies the process to make it easier to understand and uncovers the tips of building design and construction and project management. It sets up a solid foundation and fundamental framework for this field. It covers every aspect of building construction and architectural practice in plain and concise language and introduces it to all people. Through practical case studies, it demonstrates the efficient and proper ways to handle various issues and problems in architectural practice and building design and construction industry.

It is for ordinary people and aspiring young architects as well as seasoned professionals in the construction industry. For ordinary people, it uncovers the tips of building construction; for aspiring architects, it works as a construction industry survival guide and a guidebook to shorten the process in mastering architectural practice and climbing up the professional ladder; for seasoned architects, it has many checklists to refresh their memory. It is an indispensable reference book for ordinary people, architectural students, interns, drafters, designers, seasoned architects, engineers, construction administrators, superintendents, construction managers, contractors, and developers.

You will learn:
1. How to develop your business and work with your client.
2. The entire process of building design and construction, including programming, entitlement, schematic design, design development, construction documents, bidding, and construction administration.
3. How to coordinate with governing agencies, including a county's health department and a city's planning, building, fire, public works departments, etc.
4. How to coordinate with your consultants, including soils, civil, structural, electrical, mechanical, plumbing engineers, landscape architects, etc.
5. How to create and use your own checklists to do quality control of your construction documents.
6. How to use various logs (i.e., RFI log, submittal log, field visit log, etc.) and lists (contact list, document control list, distribution list, etc.) to organize and simplify your work.
7. How to respond to RFI, issue CCDs, review change orders, submittals, etc.
8. How to make your architectural practice a profitable and successful business.

Planting Design Illustrated

A Must-Have for Landscape Architecture: A Holistic Garden Design Guide with Architectural and Horticultural Insight, and Ideas from Famous Gardens in Major Civilizations

One of the most significant books on landscaping!

This is one of the most comprehensive books on planting design. It fills in the blanks of the field and introduces poetry, painting, and symbolism into planting design. It covers in detail the two major systems of planting design: formal planting design and naturalistic planting design. It has numerous line drawings and photos to illustrate the planting design concepts and principles. Through in-depth discussions of historical precedents and practical case studies, it uncovers the fundamental design principles and concepts, as well as the underpinning philosophy for planting design. It is an indispensable reference book for landscape architecture students, designers, architects, urban planners, and ordinary garden lovers.

What Others Are Saying about *Planting Design Illustrated* ...

"I found this book to be absolutely fascinating. You will need to concentrate while reading it, but the effort will be well worth your time."
—Bobbie Schwartz, former president of APLD (Association of Professional Landscape Designers) and author of *The Design Puzzle: Putting the Pieces Together*.

"This is a book that you have to read, and it is more than well worth your time. Gang Chen takes you well beyond what you will learn in other books about basic principles like color, texture, and mass."
—Jane Berger, editor & publisher of gardendesignonline

"As a longtime consumer of gardening books, I am impressed with Gang Chen's inclusion of new information on planting design theory for Chinese and Japanese gardens. Many gardening books discuss the beauty of Japanese gardens, and a few discuss the unique charms of Chinese gardens, but this one explains how Japanese and Chinese history, as well as geography and artistic traditions, bear on the development of each country's style. The material on traditional Western garden planting is thorough and inspiring, too. *Planting Design Illustrated* definitely rewards repeated reading and study. Any garden designer will read it with profit."
—Jan Whitner, editor of the *Washington Park Arboretum Bulletin*

"Enhanced with an annotated bibliography and informative appendices, *Planting Design Illustrated* offers an especially "reader friendly" and practical guide that makes it a very strongly recommended addition to personal, professional, academic, and community library gardening & landscaping reference collection and supplemental reading list."
—Midwest Book Review

"Where to start? *Planting Design Illustrated* is, above all, fascinating and refreshing! Not something the lay reader encounters every day, the book presents an unlikely topic in an easily digestible, easy-to-follow way. It is superbly organized with a comprehensive table of contents, bibliography, and appendices. The writing, though expertly informative, maintains its accessibility throughout and is a joy to read. The detailed and beautiful illustrations expanding on the concepts presented were my favorite portion. One of the finest books I've encountered in this contest in the past 5 years."
—**Writer's Digest 16th Annual International Self-Published Book Awards Judge's Commentary**

"The work in my view has incredible application to planting design generally and a system approach to what is a very difficult subject to teach, at least in my experience. Also featured is a very beautiful philosophy of garden design principles bordering poetry. It's my strong conviction that this work needs to see the light of day by being published for the use of professionals, students & garden enthusiasts."
—**Donald C. Brinkerhoff, FASLA, chairman and CEO of Lifescapes International, Inc.**

Index

Made in the USA
Lexington, KY
14 February 2015